Using UUCP and Usenet

Nutshell Handbooks

Concise, down-to-earth guides to selected UNIX topics. Some related books of interest:

Using UUCP and Usenet, 210 pp.

Shows you how to communicate with both UNIX and non-UNIX systems using UUCP and *cu*; shows you how to read news and post your own articles to other Usenet members.

Managing UUCP and Usenet, 289 pp.

For system administrators who want to install and manage the UUCP and Usenet software. As one reader noted over the Net, "Don't even TRY to install UUCP without it!"

!%@:: The Directory of Electronic Mail Addressing & Networks, 438 pp.

Answers the problem of addressing e-mail to people you've never met, on networks you've never heard of. Directory to over 130 networks around the world.

MH & xmh: E-mail for Users and Programmers, 598 pp.

Explains how to use, customize and program with the MH electronic mail commands, available on virtually any UNIX system. Packed with useful examples and tutorials.

UNIX in a Nutshell for System V or Berkeley, 296 or 272 pp.

Learning the vi Editor, 192 pp.

Learning the UNIX Operating System, 84 pp.

UNIX in a Nutshell for HyperCard, 1.8 MB

System Performance Tuning, 336 pp.

termcap & terminfo, 270 pp.

Contact us for a catalog of all our books or for orders.

O'Reilly & Associates, Inc.

Books That Help People Get More Out of Computers

632 Petaluma Avenue, Sebastopol, CA 95472
(800) 338-6887 · overseas/local (707) 829-0515 · uunet!ora!nuts

Using UUCP and Usenet

Grace Todino and Dale Dougherty

O'Reilly & Associates, Inc.
632 Petaluma Avenue
Sebastopol, CA 95472

Using UUCP and Usenet
by Grace Todino and Dale Dougherty
Nutshell Series Editor Tim O'Reilly
Copyright © 1991 O'Reilly & Associates, Inc.
All rights reserved.

Printed in the United States of America

Printing History

Feb. 1986:	First Edition; written by Grace Todino.
Nov. 1986:	Usenet sections updated to netnews 2.11 by Tim O'Reilly. Linda Lamb and Dale Dougherty.
May 1987:	Updated for Basic Networking Utilities (HoneyDanBer) UUCP, Xenix and Berkeley. Sections reorganized and expanded by Dale Dougherty. New diagrams added by Laurel Erickson. Index added. Revised page design by Linda Lamb and Dale Dougherty.
July 1987:	Minor corrections.
April 1989:	Minor corrections.
Nov. 1989:	Minor corrections.
Dec. 1989:	Minor corrections.
July 1990:	Minor corrections.
Feb. 1991:	Minor corrections.

Please address comments and questions in care of the publisher:

O'Reilly & Associates, Inc.   UUCP: uunet!ora!nuts
632 Petaluma Avenue   Internet: nuts@ora.com
Sebastopol, CA 95472
(800) 338-6887
international +1-707-829-0515

Table of Contents

Chapter 3 Executing Remote Commands

Chapter 4 Checking on UUCP Requests

Chapter 5 Logging In on a Remote System

Chapter 6 Extending the UUCP Network

Chapter 7 Using Netnews

Chapter 8 Reading News

Chapter 9 Posting News

List of Tables

Preface

Scope of This Handbook
Development of UUCP
The Nutshell Format

Using UUCP and Usenet shows you how to communicate with both UNIX and non-UNIX systems using the UUCP programs and the non-UUCP programs called **cu** and **tip**. If your site is a member of the UNIX users network (Usenet), this handbook also shows how to read news and post your own articles to other Usenet members.

In this handbook, we assume that the UUCP and Usenet links to other computer systems have already been established by your system administrator. (UUCP setup and administration is discussed in a separate Nutshell handbook, *Managing UUCP and Usenet*.) We will concentrate on describing how to perform a number of tasks allowed by these programs. At the end of this handbook, you should be able to:

☐ Send mail to a user on a remote system.
☐ Transfer files between UNIX systems.
☐ Execute commands on a remote UNIX system.
☐ Send mail and forward files to a user on a system that is not directly linked to yours.
☐ Log in to a remote UNIX or non-UNIX system while still logged into the local system.
☐ Read news articles that are broadcast by other UNIX users.
☐ Post your own articles or reply to news from other authors.

Development of UUCP

The first UUCP system was built in 1976 by Mike Lesk at AT&T Bell Laboratories as part of a research project. It became such a success that an improved version developed by Mike Lesk, David Nowitz and Greg Chesson was distributed with UNIX Version 7, and became known as **Version 2** UUCP.

With System V Release 3, AT&T began distributing a new version of UUCP that had been developed (in 1983) by Peter **Honey**man, David **A**. Nowitz and Brian **E**. Redman. They rewrote UUCP to iron out some deficiencies in Version 2, facilitate UUCP administration and provide support for more advanced communications devices and networks. This third version became popularly known as **HoneyDanBer** UUCP (derived from the authors' names) although it is more prosaically referred to as "Basic Networking Utilities" in AT&T 3B2 manuals. (Throughout this book, we will refer to this version of UUCP as BNU.) BNU is backward-compatible with Version 2, thus a UUCP network might comprise both Version 2 and BNU sites.

Many systems continue to use Version 2, including Xenix systems. Even among Version 2 sites, there are differences, though. In particular, there were some major changes to UUCP in BSD 4.3 (the latest release of Berkeley UNIX).

The differences between Version 2, BNU, and the versions of UUCP found on XENIX and Berkeley UNIX systems, by and large, do not affect the user. One improvement is worth noting, however; the newer releases do provide much improved documentation and more complete error messages. Consult the documentation shipped with your system if you find that a command or example does not work as shown in this handbook.

Which Version Do I Have?

If you don't know what version of UUCP is running on your system, check to see if your system is listed in Table 1. Which version you have is usually dependent upon the current release of UNIX that is supplied by the manufacturer. Table 1 provides a list of systems with which we are familiar, their current UNIX release and and the version of UUCP distributed with it. This list is not comprehensive, nor can it be always up-to-date. Here are a few other ways to find out which version of UUCP you have:

1. Ask your system administrator or the person who installed the UUCP software.

2. List the */usr/lib/uucp* directory.

   - If you see a file named *L.sys*, you have the "old" Version 2 UUCP.

   - If, instead, you see a file called *Systems*, then you have BNU.

3. Look it up in the UNIX documentation shipped with your system.

Table 1: UNIX-Based Systems and Current Version of UUCP

Manufacturer	Model	UNIX/UUCP Version
Apollo	3000 Series (Domain)	BSD 4.2/Version 2
Altos		Xenix/Version 2
AT&T	3B1 (UNIX PC)	Sys. V.2/Version 2
	3B2	Sys. V.3/BNU
	3B15	Sys. V.3/BNU
Convergent	Miniframe (CTIX)	Sys. V.2/Version 2
Technologies	Mightyframe (CTIX)	Sys. V.3/BNU
Digital	MicroVAX	Ultrix/Version 2 Plus
	VAX	BSD 4.3/Version 2 Plus
Encore	Multimax	Sys. V.3/BNU
IBM	RT-PC (AIX)	Sys. V.2/Version 2
Masscomp	MC-5000 Series	Sys. V.3/BNU
Microport	PC/AT	Sys V.2/Version 2

Table 1: UNIX-Based Systems and Current Version of UUCP

Manufacturer	Model	UNIX/UUCP Version
NCR	Tower 32/16	Sys. V.2/Version 2
Prime	EXL Series	Sys. V.3/BNU
Pyramid	90x	BSD 4.2/Version 2
SCO/XENIX	PC/XT	SysV.2/Version 2
Unisys	5000 Series (NCR)	Sys. V.2/BNU
Unisys	5000 Series (Arix)	Sys. V.3/BNU
Unisys	6000 Series	Sys. V.3/BNU
Unisys	7000 Series	Sys. V.2/Version 2

The Nutshell Format

The UUCP programs often get lost in the large listing of UNIX programs found in the *UNIX Reference Manuals*. Probably their sole identification is that they are all named "uu ...". The programs and procedures for using Usenet are not even included in the standard UNIX documentation, except on Berkeley systems. What we have done here is to compile information about the UUCP and Usenet programs in one handbook to get you working with them right away.

The following sections describe the conventions used in this handbook.

Commands

The commands are described according to the tasks they perform. When the syntax of a command is given, as in the following example:

uucp [*option*] *source dest*

the items that you, the user, would type in as shown are printed in **boldface**. Those items that you supply are shown in *italics*, and those that are in brackets [] are optional. For example, the proper way to use the **uucp** command is to enter the word "uucp" followed by an option (if desired), the name of the *source* file and the *dest*ination file.

Examples

We have included several examples to show the results that you can expect when you type in a command. The examples are not meant to be typed in since they assume that the files shown already exist.

Examples are set off from the main text in smaller type. Items that a user following the example would enter are shown in **boldface**. System messages and responses are shown in normal type.

An example would appear as follows:

```
% uuname
newyork
calif
%
```

The local system prompt is "%". The user would enter "uuname" and then press the RETURN key. The system responds by printing "newyork" and "calif," and then giving another prompt.

Note to Our Readers

We see each Nutshell Handbook as reflecting the experience of a group of users. They're not written by "experts," but by people who have gone through a similar learning process as you. Our goal is to share what we know from experience so that you can become more productive in less time.

As publishers, this goal is reflected in the way we maintain the series by updating each title periodically. This allows us to incorporate changes suggested to us by our readers. We'd like new users to benefit from *your* experience as well as ours.

If you have a suggestion or solve a significant problem that our handbook does not cover, please write to us and let us know about it. Include information about the UNIX environment in which you work and the particular machine you use. If we are able to use your suggestion in the next edition of the book, we will send you a copy of the new edition. You'll have our thanks, along with the thanks of future readers of this handbook.

1

An Introduction to UUCP

A Communications Network
Overview of UUCP User Programs
A Sample UUCP Network
Identifying Remote Systems
Sending Mail to Remote Systems
The USENET Network

In this chapter, we'll introduce a few basic concepts essential to using a UUCP communications network of UNIX systems. We will take our first look at the programs that are part of this facility, and the functions that they perform. We'll show you how to find out which remote systems you can contact and how to send mail to users on those systems.

A Communications Network

Using a communications network is a common convenience for most of us. It allows people at different locations to exchange information. Think of communicating without one in place. What if your telephone could only be used as an intercom for in-house calls? What if your letters could only be sent through inter-departmental mail and not through the post office? The mail and telephone networks are practically global in reach.

A communications network for computers is typically limited to the connections established between several *remote* systems. Such connections might span a distance of three feet or three thousand miles.

With a communications network, users of different computer systems can share information just as users of the same system can. Users can transfer files between systems and utilize resources unique to each system.

A communications link is the product of hardware connections and software programs. A physical connection must be made between the systems for sending and receiving data. The physical connection might be a cable used to connect two systems at the same site. Or it might require a modem for communications across phone lines to distant sites. Once these connections are in place, software is needed to conduct the operations of the network on each of the systems. And that is where UUCP comes in.

UUCP is a networking facility for the UNIX operating system. Its software consists of files and programs for configuring and administering this facility and a number of programs that give users access to it. In this handbook, we will concentrate on the programs intended for UUCP users. (UUCP refers to this facility; the **uucp** program is part of this facility and stands for *U*nix-to-*U*nix *C*opy). With UUCP, you can:

- Send mail to users on a remote system.

- Transfer files between UNIX systems.

- Access resources of a remote computer system.

There are a variety of ways to apply UUCP. Let's look at three different situations.

1. In a small business, there are several minicomputer systems but only one laser printer. They use UUCP to send files for printing on the system that is connected to the laser printer.

2. A chain of retail stores has a UNIX system on-site at each store to collect data from electronic cash registers. At night, UUCP transfers the files containing the information about that day's business to a larger UNIX computer for processing at the central office.

3. Programmers working at several different sites are working on a large programming project. Members of this project team use UUCP to exchange updated source files, as well as to send messages to each other throughout the course of the project.

Of course, all these activities require some degree of cooperation from the remote system and its users.

Overview of UUCP User Programs

Once a UUCP communications network is in place, there are a number of programs that you can use. Some are standard UNIX programs that can also be used with UUCP, and others are more specifically a part of the UUCP facility.

Here are two standard UNIX programs that can be used on a UUCP network:

- **mail**, UNIX's messaging facility, can be used to send mail messages to users on a remote system.

- **cu** (or **tip** on Berkeley systems) can be used to login to a remote system, providing that you have been assigned a login name and password on that system.

In addition, UUCP provides five main programs for the user to work with:

- **uucp**, which is used to request a file transfer to or from a remote machine. It works much like **cp**, with added syntax for addressing remote machines.

- **uux**, which is used to request execution of a command on a remote machine. The commands that can be executed are usually limited, for security reasons, but might include, for instance, printing on a printer attached to a remote machine.

- **uuname**, which is used to list the names of other systems that are connected to your system.

- **uulog** and **uustat**, which are used to get information on the status of **uucp** or **uux** requests.

Versions of UUCP shipped with System V support the additional user programs **uuto** and **uupick**. **uuto** is a shell script that let you send files to a user on another machine by addressing the files to the user by name (*a la* **mail**). **uupick** is the corresponding script that is used to pick up files sent with **uuto**.

Berkeley 4.3 systems include the additional programs **uuq** and **uusend**. **uuq** lets you view and manipulate UUCP jobs that are waiting to be processed. **uusend** allows you to forward files through a string of systems. (This same feature is supported by **uucp** itself in certain System V implementations of UUCP.)

There is quite a bit more complexity behind the scenes (which presumably, your system administrator understands). A background program, or daemon, called **uucico** actually does most of the work transferring files or remote execution requests back and forth between systems. (Sometimes, it will appear in a list of your processes if you do a **ps** after having entered a UUCP command.) There are also quite a few data files that need to be in place, giving information on the systems to be called and the mechanisms to be used to place the call. To learn more about how UUCP works, consult the companion handbook, *Managing UUCP and Usenet*.

The UUCP programs are straightforward and easy to use once you are used to the conventions. However, we'd like to offer some general advice about using UUCP:

1. *Patience, patience — UUCP will get around to it.*

   The results of a UUCP command are not always immediate. UUCP is a batch processing network. That is, a user makes a request and the UUCP programs carry it out in due time. You may have already encountered such a situation if you share a printer among a group of users. Once you make a print request, your file is spooled and printed when the printer becomes available and your request is next in the queue.

   When a UUCP job is entered, it is spooled for later transmission. It may happen that the request is carried out immediately, but often it does not. Sometimes, when UUCP tries to carry out the request, the remote system is not available and the request will fail. However, UUCP, like the proverbial salesman, will try, try again to contact the system and eventually the request will succeed.

2. *You can't always get what you want.*

Access to remote files and commands is usually limited. Unlimited access is seldom given any user, whether local or remote. The system administrator of each system in the network determines the privileges of remote users. After some experience, you will usually find out what commands you can and cannot execute or in what directories you can and cannot go for files.

You may experience difficulty in sending or retrieving a file because you do not have permission to read or write to that file. In particular, the number of commands that can be executed on one UNIX system by another is typically very small. This is a security feature to prevent unauthorized access by a remote user.

3. *Expect some frustration.*

Think of waiting in long lines at the post office to buy stamps. Or dialing a number that's always busy. You can expect to encounter similar frustration using UUCP. Devices fail; lines get wacky; logins get changed, etc. When you are stuck in traffic, in a growing backlog of UUCP requests, you may not always be able to help yourself. The system administrator should (or will) come to expect your frequent three-alarm calls for help. Keep on good terms with anyone who has continued success getting through.

A Sample UUCP Network

Let us look at a hypothetical UUCP network consisting of five UNIX systems, as shown in Figure 1-1.

You can think of this network on a city/state scheme. The local system (our point of reference) is called *newton* (a suburb of Boston). It is hardwired at 9600 baud to system *waltham*. A *hardwired connection* (or direct link) consists of a local cable or leased line that connects two systems.

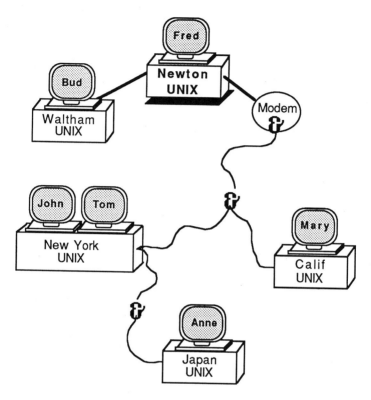

Figure 1-1. An Example of a Network

Fred is a user on the local system and Bud is a user on the remote system *waltham*.

newton is further linked to *newyork, calif,* and *japan* using a phone link at 1200 baud. A *phone connection* (or remote link) typically involves a phone line, a device called a *modem* connected to one of the system's terminal ports, and a system with *dial-out* capability. Dial-out capability enables it to call another system. The modem (short for *mo*dulator-*dem*odulator) converts the binary codes used by the computer into tones that can be transmitted over the telephone lines. These tones must be decoded by another modem on the other end. In the example above, systems *calif* and *newyork* are both linked to *newton* via phone lines. Thus, Fred can communicate with Mary and Tom. Fred can also communicate with Anne, a user on the remote system *japan*. To do this, he has to forward his message through the remote system *newyork.*

In addition, there are high-speed local area network connections (LAN), such as Ethernet, which consist of add-on hardware devices and software. A network might include direct, dialout, and LAN links and provide access to many different remote systems.

Each remote system may have certain access times or privileges unique to that system and set up by your system administrator. For instance, your system might limit network activity to evening hours. Or your system might be set up as a passive system that waits for the remote system to contact it and never initiates contact on its own. If you are a passive system, the other system might agree to poll your system on a regular basis, such as every night, to see if there are any work requests. In these cases, UUCP will hold on to your request until the time is right.

A UNIX communications network is typically made up of a diverse group of machines. While each of the systems run the UNIX operating system (or a derivative), the machines are seldom all made by the same manufacturer. For instance, one of the systems could be an IBM PC-XT running XENIX, another an IBM PC-AT running Microport's System V/AT, while other larger systems might be an AT&T 3B2/310 running System V Release 3, an NCR Tower running System V Release 2, and a DEC VAX running Berkeley 4.3.

Although each of these systems runs UNIX and supports UUCP, there are differences from one implementation to the next that can affect how commands perform from system to system. As always, if you run into problems, consult the documentation shipped with your system.

Identifying Remote Systems

Each system on a UUCP network has a file that describes the remote systems to which it is linked. This file is created by the system administrator of each system and identifies each remote system by name.

You can use the **uuname** command to find out the name of your own system and the names of remote systems to which you have a link.

uuname In A Nutshell

---

uuname [*option*]

Print the names of remote systems connected to the local system.

option

    -l   print the local system's name.

---

uuname has only one option. The **-l** (for local) option displays the network name for your own system:

```
% uuname -l
newton
%
```

This means that the local system is known as *newton* to other UNIX systems.

The **uuname** command, without any arguments, lists the names of all systems known by UUCP. In our hypothetical network as shown in Figure 1, the **uuname** command would display the following output:

```
% uuname
waltham
newyork
calif
%
```

If the list is longer than your screen, pipe the **uuname** output through the **pg** or **more** program. If the system you want to talk to is not on the list, you should see the system administrator about setting up an additional link to that system.

And Mark It With ! (or \!)

To use the remote system in a command, you need to specify the system name followed by an exclamation mark(!). What follows the exclamation mark will be interpreted by the remote system.

    systemname![*username* | *pathname*]

When used in a command, the remote *systemname* is followed by the name of a user on that system or a path locating a particular file or directory on that system.

Users of the C-shell know that the exclamation mark has a special use (for **history**); therefore it must be escaped with a backslash.

system\![*username* | *pathname*]

Because the C-shell syntax also works in the Bourne shell (the backslash is ignored), we will continue to use it in our examples throughout this book.

Sending Mail to Remote Systems

Once you know that a link exists, and have its name, you can easily send a mail message to users on the remote system. In general, mail can be sent to any user on any system on the **uuname** list. If the recipient does not exist, the mail will be returned to you along with the message "**User unknown.**"

There are several different mail programs available in UNIX. System V has two programs: **mail** is a very simple mail program, while **mailx** is an implementation of the more powerful Berkeley **mail** program. In this section, we'll use the simple System V **mail** program. In Chapter 6, *Extending the UUCP Network*, we'll look at the **mailx** (Berkeley **mail**) environment in more detail.

To send mail over UUCP, you supply a system name before the user's login id:

Providing that there is a UUCP connection to *newyork*, you can send mail to user *tom* on that system. Here's the **mail** command and the message:

```
% mail newyork\!tom

I am testing out our UUCP link.
Please send me mail when you receive this message.

Fred
^D
```

To emphasize a point made earlier about UUCP in general, you can't expect the mail message to get there immediately. If you were sending mail to a directly connected system in the same building, the message might get there in a few minutes. But since a message to *newyork* requires a long-distance phone call, the administrator may have set up UUCP to place calls to *newyork* only in the evening, when telephone rates are cheaper. You can then expect the message to be delivered overnight. Let's say that you send the mail on Wednesday. On Thursday, when Tom logs in, he gets your message.

```
From uucp Thu Jan 30 8:49 EST 1987
>From fred Wed Jan 29 10:56 EST 1987 remote from newton
Status: R


I am testing out our UUCP link.
Please send me mail when you receive this message.

Fred
```

As you can see, **mail** provides a header that identifies the sender and the remote system.

If you send mail to a user that doesn't exist on a remote system, or to a remote system that is not connected to yours, UUCP will send mail that informs you of this error.

Once Tom has received the message from Fred, he can send a reply.

```
% mail newton\!fred

I got your message this morning.  Why not
try to send that report you've been
promising me?

Tom
^D
%
```

Sending a File Through the Mail

The **mail** facility offers an easy way to send a file to a user on another system. The shell's input redirection symbol (<) is used to include the file.

```
% mail newyork\!tom < report
```

The file, here named *report*, will be sent to the user and appear in his or her mail. The recipient can then save it in a file.

While you can transfer files through the mail facility, there are some disadvantages for general use. A long mail message, such as might be generated by a sizable file, might catch a user by surprise. It can be difficult to read the header information because the message scrolls right past you. In addition, the user has to delete the header information supplied by **mail** once the file has been saved. The **uucp** or **uuto** commands, as shown in the next chapter, are preferable for file transfer.

Mail Forwarding

You can further increase the scope of a local mail network through a mechanism called *forwarding*. For instance, if you were on *newton*, you can send mail to *japan*, which is linked to *newyork* but not to you.

```
% mail newyork\!japan\!anne

I'm using the UNIX mail facility to send
you a message via UUCP.  If you get
this message, please reply to me at the
following address:   newyork!newton!fred
```

The above mail message will be sent to *newyork*; this system will then send it on to *japan*.

You can even go further and send mail to a user on *japan*'s neighbor. You can set up as many forwarding links to your final destination as long as the systems on the link agree to forward your mail or your files.

We'll look at other details of forwarding in Chapter 6, *Extending the UUCP Network*, in the section "Beyond the Local Network." The point we'd like to make here, though, is that forwarding extends the boundaries of your local network and allows you to reach other systems not directly connected to yours.

The UUCP network currently consists of thousands of UNIX installations worldwide, and they can be reached if you know the network pathname to them. Your link to the UNIX network becomes your link to the world and the world's link to you.

The Usenet Network

Usenet (for *"user's net*work") is a collection of UNIX systems that runs the **netnews** software. The net (as it is commonly called) is a public forum for the exchange of ideas in the form of news articles that are broadcast to member sites. Net users can post articles, forward mail, send followup articles to previous articles, or simply read the news using the **netnews** programs.

More than anything, it is the people who give much of the flavor and color to the net.

Although net interaction is not face-to-face, it is personal, and over the years certain rules of conduct have evolved. They are described in a document called *Net Etiquette*, which should be available from the system administrator at each site on the net.

netnews is not part of standard UNIX (like UUCP), but many of the systems that belong to the net use UUCP. (Others are connected by ARPANET or various local networks.) Each system on the net has a file set up by the system administrator which describes the systems that will send the news to your site, the type of news that is received, the systems that will broadcast your news, and the type of links available. All that you need to know in order to read news is the program and the type of article you want to read.

Posting news is a little more complicated and requires following certain rules laid down in *Net Etiquette*. You need to determine how widely you want to distribute your news, and if you're replying by mail, you need to know the net address of the author.

The net address often includes a major news exchange, sometimes referred to as a *backbone site*. A backbone site is loosely defined as a site which serves as a major feed to a geographical or organizational region. For example, *ucbvax* is the main feed to the University of California at Berkeley. Both are backbone sites.

You can think of a backbone site as the center of a web, with local networks growing into and out of it. News that is sent to a backbone site is passed on to other backbone sites as quickly as possible, so that it gets transmitted over a wide area in a short time. At the time of this writing (September 1989), 90% of all **netnews** postings have been transmitted all over North America within two hours after being posted. That's fast!

The net is a non-commercial network. There is no one person or organization that administers the thousands of member sites worldwide; every user is expected to police his or her own actions. The volume of news on the net can get to be staggering, so some sites have limited the number and type of news articles they subscribe to.

When used properly, the net is a unique way to stay informed and up-to-date on categories from UNIX to politics. When you use Usenet, you don't just receive news; you interact with it.

2

File Transfer

Accessing Remote File Systems
Using the Public Directory
Using **uucp**
Filename Metacharacters and Pathnames
Beyond the PUBDIR
Determining the Status of a File Transfer
Make It Easy on Yourself

This chapter demonstrates how to transfer files between networked UNIX systems. Sending files to a remote system, or retrieving them, is perhaps the most frequently utilized function of UUCP. The commands for transferring files are easy to learn, but restricted access to directories on a remote file system can make it difficult for a transfer to succeed. To get around these security restrictions, UNIX systems employ a public directory which anyone can access.

Two commands are designed specifically for conducting file transfers between the public directory on the local and remote systems. These commands are **uuto** and **uupick** and are as simple to use as the mail facility. However, they are not available on all UNIX systems. The **uucp** program is the general file transfer utility of UUCP. You can use **uucp** to attempt transferring files to any location on a remote file system.

Accessing Remote File Systems

A UUCP connection consists of some type of communications link between two UNIX systems. Because of that connection, users are able to copy files between systems just as they copy files between directories. Here's the **cp** command:

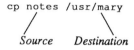

```
cp notes /usr/mary
```
Source   Destination

This command makes a copy of the file *notes* (from the current working directory) and places it in the directory */usr/mary* on the same (local) system. Here's the **uucp** command:

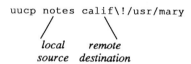

```
uucp notes calif\!/usr/mary
```
local   remote
source   destination

This command sends a copy of the file to the remote system *calif* where *notes* will be placed in the */usr/mary* directory there. (As we'll discuss shortly, file permissions may not permit UUCP to copy the file into this directory.) You can also copy a remote source file to a local destination. We'll look at the **uucp** command in more detail later on.

To identify a *remote system* in a UUCP command, you must include the system name. (You can get a list of the remote systems that are connected to your system with the **uuname** command, as explained in the last chapter.) A system name precedes the pathname of the file or directory and is separated from it by an exclamation point (!). If you are using the C shell, remember to escape the exclamation mark with a backslash.

When you send a file to a remote system, you may have problems getting past the security set up to protect that file system. (See the accompanying box "File System Security.") Undoubtedly, you have already encountered the same difficulty on your own system when you try to copy a file to a restricted directory. Look at the following example:

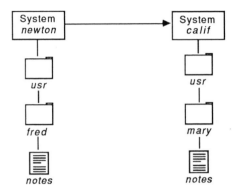

```
uucp notes calif\!/usr/mary
```

Figure 2-1. Sending a File from *newton* to *calif*

```
% cp test /bin
cp: cannot create /bin/test
                  /
        need write permission
          in this directory
```

Because the user does not have permission to write a file to the /bin
directory, the cp command fails. It would also fail if the directory that
you specified did not exist.

The same kinds of problems that occur when copying files with cp can
happen when you attempt a file transfer. However, when cp fails, you
get a message immediately. Unfortunately, when UUCP fails, you
don't always know about it until you go searching for an answer.

In preparing to transfer a file, you need to know more than the remote
system's name; you need to decide where you are going to put the file
on that system.

The system administrator at each site sets up a special file that
describes the kind of access that remote users are allowed. For security reasons, the system administrator usually decides to limit access to

certain parts of a filesystem. Dialup access is often very restricted, while access between two hardwired systems in a local network may be less restricted. Therefore, you can't always count on being able to transfer a file to any location on a remote file system. However, that doesn't mean you can't get it there.

To avoid problems with filesystem access, you can use a special directory that is accessible by everyone. The *Public Directory* is available to both local and remote users for sending and receiving files. The full pathname to this directory is *usr/spool/uucppublic*, an annoyingly long name to type (remember there are two *p*'s). Use of this public directory increases the chances that any file transfer will succeed.

We'll start off showing you how to send files to the Public Directory. Then we'll look at transferring files between non-public directories, and what you need to know to improve your chances of success.

Using the Public Directory

System administrators have the option of restricting incoming and outgoing UUCP file transfers to the the public directory (sometimes called PUBDIR.)

The pathname of PUBDIR is */usr/spool/uucppublic*. Let's take a look at the structure of the PUBDIR on *newton*:

PUBDIR may contain files and subdirectories. In our example above, PUBDIR contains a file called *file* and the subdirectories *receive*, *fred*, and *alice*. *receive* is a fairly standard subdirectory on UUCP and is used to hold files sent by the **uuto** command that will be described later. The subdirectories *alice*, and *fred* correspond to the login IDs of users on system *newton*. *PUBDIR/fred* can be used by user *fred* to hold files that can be copied by remote users, and it is used by remote users to send files to *fred*. Sending files to PUBDIR is the safest and easiest way to copy a file (and often the only way). UUCP also places files in this directory when a file transfer to a non-public directory fails.

There are three commands you can use when copying a file to and from PUBDIR: **uucp**, **uuto** and **uupick**. **uuto** and **uupick** (System V only) are more useful for novice users since they allow users to copy files without having to spell out a pathname. **uuto** and **uupick** commands

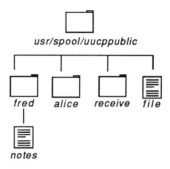

usr/spool/uucppublic

fred   alice   receive   file

notes

Figure 2-2. Structure of Public Directory

are not available on all systems. If you don't have them on your system, you might want to skip ahead to read about **uucp**. However, you may want to look at the syntax for **uuto**, as it is a shell script that invokes **uucp**. If you prefer this interface, you should be able to construct a local version of **uuto**.

Using **uuto** and **uupick** (System V)

The **uuto** command delivers a local source file to the PUBDIR on the remote system, and notifies the recipient by **mail** when the file arrives. Any file sent by **uuto** can be retrieved by the remote user from the public directory with the command **uupick**.

File System Security
—You Can Bank on It!

Imagine trying to put something into or take something out of a safe deposit box at a bank. All's well and good as long as you are at your own bank, where the guard presumably knows you and permits you to enter the vault. Once inside, you use a combination or key to open (and empty, if you wish) the safe deposit box that has been assigned to you.

Now what happens when you want to give some of your baubles and bangles to a friend who wants to store them in his own safe deposit box at another bank. How do you go about this, especially when it's not convenient for both of you to do this together?

Well, you know that he can't just walk into to your bank and remove them from your safe deposit box. Similarly, you couldn't take them to his bank and place them in his safe deposit box. You could give him the key to your box—you're going to trust him with your baubles and bangles, aren't you? Presuming that he finds his way to your bank, chances are that he might not be permitted to enter the vault—the guard knows you, not him and the bank doesn't want your friend wandering around. The security is responsible for protecting all the safe deposit boxes.

Here's a reasonable solution to this dilemma. Remove the goods from your safe deposit box and go to his bank. Make sure you get directions and that you go when the bank is open. Now, instead of trying to enter the vault, leave them with a teller for your friend to pick up when he arrives. He can place these precious jewels in his safe deposit box himself.

This is the rationale for using the public directory as an intermediary for file transfers. Generally, you won't have a problem getting the file to the remote system. But you will be turned away if you try to place the file in a protected directory.

In the last chapter, we demonstrated how to send mail to a user on a remote system. With the **mail** command, you supplied the name by which the remote system is known to your system and the name by which the remote user is known on his or her system. With **uuto**, you use this syntax but also supply the name of a local file that you want to send to that user.

Here's what you enter to send mail to user *john* on the remote system *newyork*.

```
% mail newyork!john
```
　　　　/
　　Name of remote system
　　and user's login ID

And here's what you enter to send a file to the same destination using **uuto**.

```
% uuto file newyork!john
```
　　　/
　pathname of file
　on local system

uuto is a shell script that uses the three pieces of information that you supply (filename, system name, and user id of the recipient) to build a **uucp** command. It generates a pathname for the file that will place it in the public directory on the remote system.

For example, if *mary*, a user on the system named *calif*, were to send the file *target_list* from her working directory to the user *fred* at *newton*, she would type:

```
% uuto target_list newton!fred
```

When this file arrives at *newton*, it can be found in PUBDIR with the following pathname:

```
/usr/spool/uucppublic/receive/fred/calif/target_list
```
　　　　　│　　　　　　　　　│　　│　　　　　　│
　public directory　　　　*userid*　*system*　　*filename*

uuto In A Nutshell

---

uuto [*options*] *file(s) system*\!*userid*

Send a file to the public directory of a remote system.

options

-m   Notify sender through mail that copy was successful.

-p   Copy specified files into the spool directory before sending them to the remote system.

file(s)   pathname of one or more files to send from the local system to the remote system.

system   name of a remote system.

userid   login name of the remote user who will receive the copy.

---

receive is a subdirectory of the public directory that is used by **uuto**, *userid* is the recipient's login name, *system* is the name of remote system from which the file originated, and *filename* is the name given to the file.

In addition, the recipient (*fred*) is notified by mail with a message similar to this:

```
From uucp  Fri May 25 14:51 EDT 1987
/usr/spool/uucppublic/receive/fred/calif/test from
calif!mary arrived
```

Sender of file

John could copy or move this file from the public directory to any place on the filesystem that he has permission to write. You can do this directly with the **mv** command or use the **uupick** command.

When you invoke **uupick**, it looks for a file that was sent by **uuto**. (You cannot pick files sent by **uucp** (without **uuto**) unless they were sent with the pathname: */usr/spool/uucppublic/receive/user/system* .) When it finds such a file, it prints the file's name, origin, and whether it is a file or directory. It then prompts you for action on the terminal screen. There are a handful of commands, allowing you to move the file into your current directory or delete it. At the question mark prompt, press **q** to quit without taking any action. Or press **m** to move

uupick In A Nutshell

---

uupick [*option*] [*file*]

Retrieve files from public directory that were sent to you from a remote system via the **uuto** command.

-s*sys*   Pick up files sent from a given *system*.

If no option is given, all files sent using **uuto** can be picked up. You can also specify the name of the file if you know what it is.

Interactive Commands

You are prompted (?) to respond for each file of yours in the public directory. Pressing RETURN at the prompt will go to the next file, or if none, quits program.

    *   List interactive commands.

    d   Delete the file without copying it.

    m [*dir*]
          Move the file into the current or specified directory.

    a [*dir*]
          Move all files from the same system into current or specified directory.

    p   Print the contents of the file on the terminal screen.

    q   Quit.

    ^D   (Control-D) Quit.

    !cmd Escape to shell to run command.

---

the file into your current working directory. For instance,

```
% uupick
remote from system calif: file target_list
?
m <Return>
7 blocks
%
```

target_list is moved into the John's current directory. A message gives the size of this file in blocks.

If there is more than one file for you, you will be prompted to respond for each one. Pressing $\boxed{\text{RETURN}}$ will display the name of the next file; if there are no more files for you, pressing $\boxed{\text{RETURN}}$ will take you out of the program. You can use the **-s** option when you invoke **uupick** if you want to limit the files selected to those from a particular system.

Using uucp

The syntax of the **uucp** command differs from **uuto** in that it requires you to specify the pathname of the file on the remote system. **uucp** was designed to be as similar as possible in form and use to the UNIX **cp** ("*copy*") command. They have virtually the same syntax, except that **uucp** allows you to transfer files between systems. (You can learn the names of remote systems connected to your system by entering the **uuname** command.) Either the *source* or the *destination* can include the name of a remote system.

Sending to the Public Directory

When you transfer files to the public directory of a remote system using **uucp**, you must supply the full pathname.

If user *fred* wanted to copy the file *plans* from his working directory to the PUBDIR of system *calif*, he would type:

```
% uucp plans calif\!/usr/spool/uucppublic/plans.fred
```
                    /
            full pathname
         of public directory

The file *plans* will be copied from the local system to the system *calif* and placed in the public directory. The new file will be named *plans.fred*.

Because */usr/spool/uucppublic* is a long pathname to type, there is a special notation for referring to PUBDIR in a **uucp** command. The tilde character followed by a slash (˜/) will be interpreted as */usr/spool/uucppublic*. Thus, the above example can be shortened to:

uucp In A Nutshell

> ### **uucp** [*option*] *source destination*
>
> Make a copy of a file, where the *source* or *destination* of that file is a pathname on a local or remote system.
>
> *options*   The following options are generally useful for basic purposes. See Appendix E, *Quick Reference*, for additional options.
>
> -C   Copy the local *source* file to the spool directory before attempting transfer. Normally, it uses a pointer to retrieve the file.
>
> -f   Do not make new parent directories to copy file. Normally, it tries to create directories that do not exist.
>
> -j   Display UUCP job request number.
>
> -m   Notify sender by mail when copy is completed.
>
> -n*user*
>   Notify *user* on remote system by mail when file arrives.
>
> -r   Queue the job, but do not contact remote system immediately.
>
> -s*file*   Send messages about status of file transfer to *file*; supply absolute pathname of file.
>
> *source*   the pathname of the file or files you want to copy. If preceded by a system name, UUCP will try to retrieve that file from a remote system.
>
> *destination*
>   the pathname of the directory or file where the copy will be placed. If preceded by a system name, UUCP will try to send that file to a remote system.
>
> *Abbreviated Pathname for Public Directory:* ˜/*filename*

```
% uucp plans calif\!˜/plans.fred
                       \
                 tilde-slash
              represents PUBDIR
```

~/plans.fred is expanded to */usr/spool/uucppublic/plans.fred* at system *calif*. If you use the C shell, see the section "Filename Metacharacters and Pathnames" below; the tilde character has special meaning in the C shell and must be quoted or escaped in a **uucp** command.

The local source file must have read permissions for all users in order for UUCP to copy the file. Here's what happens when UUCP can't read a file:

```
% ls -l spider
-rw-rw----  1 fred    doc    264 Feb  5 17:35 spider

% uucp spider calif~/
can't read file (/usr/fred/book/spider) mode (100660)
uucp failed partially: 1 error
```

Use the **chmod** command to change the permissions of files. Any file transferred by UUCP will end up with 0666 permissions (readable and writable by owner, group, and all others); and *uucp* will own the file. For more on file permissions, see the section "Beyond the PUBDIR" below.

Let's look at another example in which we send a file to a subdirectory off the public directory.

```
% uucp report calif\!~/mary
```

You will get two different results depending upon whether or not there already is a directory named */usr/spool/uucppublic/mary* on the remote system. If there is, the file *reports* will be placed in it. If the directory does not exist, then the file will be named *mary* in */usr/spool/uucppublic*. You can make sure that *mary* is a directory by putting a slash (/) at the end of the destination pathname. Thus, we could enter the above command as such:

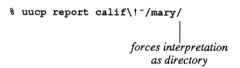

*forces interpretation
as directory*

This ensures that *report* will end up as a file in the directory */usr/spool/uucppublic/mary*. UUCP will create the directory if it does not exist.

"I did it and it failed"

Using **UUCP** takes some getting used to, and as we said earlier, it takes patience. Error messages that appear immediately after you enter the command usually have to do with syntax errors, typos or problems accessing a local file. The most common error message is:

```
% uucp calif\!~/mary/
usage uucp from ... to
uucp failed completely
```

In this instance, only one pathname was supplied. Look at the following example, entered in the C shell:

```
% uucp report calif\!~/mary/
bad system name: calif
uucp failed completely (code -4)
% !!:p
uucp report ^Hcalif\!~/mary/
```

The **history** mechanism in the C shell allows us to look at the command again and notice that the problem was caused by an inadvertent backspace character. To all appearances, it looked as though we had typed the command correctly.

Once you enter the command, **uucp** does try to verify that it knows the remote system that you named, but it obviously cannot immediately verify whether the pathname of a remote file or directory is a valid one.

If you get no immediate error message, and your system prompt reappears, then your **uucp** command went through and the file transfer has been queued for processing.

UUCP uses a spooling system, that is, it collects requests in a queue and acts on them as devices and lines are available. Sometimes, it cannot carry out the request because the phone line is busy or the remote system is down. But it will hold on to the request and try again.

So, if a file transfer does not appear to be immediately successful, **do not repeat the uucp command!** All that you will accomplish is to put another request in the queue.

Up ahead in this chapter, we'll look at some programs for checking on the progress of your request and, again, in Chapter 4, *Checking on UUCP Requests*, when we'll look at some of the problems that can and do arise in file transfers.

Retrieving Files from a Remote Public Directory

You can use the **uucp** command to get a file from a remote system. In this case, the *source* is on the remote system and the *destination* is on the local system.

For instance, the owner of a remote system is reluctant to incur phone charges for sending you a large file. Instruct that person to place the file in the public directory on their system. Then you should be able to take it off their system without any trouble. (File system security can make it difficult to get a file from non-public directories.)

Most users place public files in their own subdirectory of PUBDIR so that they are easily accessible by remote users. If *mary* placed the file *notes* in her subdirectory of PUBDIR at system *calif*, *fred* could copy the file to the PUBDIR at system *newton* by typing:

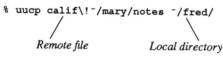

```
% uucp calif\!~/mary/notes ~/fred/
```
        Remote file   *Local directory*

The file is copied to a directory named *fred* in the local PUBDIR. (If you use the C shell, this example will work differently, as explained in the section "Filename Metacharacters and Pathnames"; it will try to place the remote file in a subdirectory *fred* off of *fred*'s login directory.)

Notifying Users of File Transfer

Two of the more useful **uucp** options notify the sender or receiver of the file copy when the transfer is complete. Notifying the sender is a useful way to learn that a request has succeeded. Notifying the recipient tells him or her that the file has arrived and where to find it.

Notifying the Sender

The **-m** flag tells **uucp** or **uuto** to notify you (the sender) when a copy is done. This option does not work if you are retrieving multiple files from a remote system. Here are several examples, assuming that *newton* is the local system:

```
% uucp -m calif\!~/mary/plans ~/fred/myplans
% uucp -m plans ideas budget calif\!~/mary
% uuto -m test waltham\!~/bud
```

The first example retrieves a single file called *plans* from the system *calif* and renames it *myplans* in the subdirectory of *fred* in the public directory on the local system. The second example sends the files *plans*, *ideas* and *budget* to the subdirectory *mary* in the public directory on *calif*. The third example sends the file *test* from the local directory to the *bud* subdirectory of PUBDIR on *waltham*. In all the examples, the **-m** flag would notify you when the file transfers were complete.

The mail message that you would see for the last example is shown below:

```
From uucp Fri May 25 10:38 EDT 1987
file /usr/fred/test, system waltham
copy succeeded
```

Notifying the Recipient

When you use the **uuto** command, the recipient is automatically notified of the file transfer. That is because you supply the user's name on the command line and **uuto** supplies it as the **-n***user* option to **uucp**.

With the **-n***user* option, **uucp** sends mail to the recipient of the file on the other system when the copy is complete. It can be especially useful in situations where the user is not expecting to receive a file. For example:

```
% uucp -m -nmary plans calif\!~mary/mktg/plans
```

Recipient's login id

notifies both you and *mary* by **mail** of a successful copy.

Moving Files Out of the Public Directory

It's a good idea to move the files in */usr/spool/uucppublic* to a private directory as soon as possible. UUCP administrative shell scripts may periodically delete files in this directory.

You can use the **mv** command to place these files in the current working directory.

```
% mv /usr/spool/uucppublic/mary/* .
```

Or you may want to use a shell script similar to **uupick** to retrieve these files. One such script, called **uuset**, is demonstrated at the end of this chapter and is listed in Appendix A, *Useful Shell Scripts*. **uuget** allows you to "get" files from the public directory and place them elsewhere on the filesystem.

Filename Metacharacters and Pathnames

This section discusses a number of specific problems, often related to the intervention of the shell, that occur in naming files in a **uucp** command.

One of the functions of the shell is to evaluate and expand filenames that appear on a command line. In a **uucp** command, problems can arise when you use filename metacharacters in a remote pathname. You want the metacharacter expanded on the remote system, not on your own.

This is not really a problem in the Bourne shell, as it "knows" not to expand the filename metacharacters "*****", "**?**", and "**[ ]**" in a remote pathname.

The C shell is not so "smart." Users of the C shell should put metacharacters within quotes if they appear in a remote pathname.

In the C Shell, the tilde character (˜) is normally expanded to the user's login directory if it appears at the beginning of an argument. Thus, **ls ˜** will list the contents of your home directory; **ls ˜fred** will list Fred's login directory. If you want a tilde interpreted as the path of the public directory in a **uucp** command, put it inside quotes or escape it with a backslash. In the next section, we'll look at some examples that demonstrate commands with and without quoted metacharacters.

You can use absolute or relative pathnames when referring to local files. When you supply a relative pathname, **uucp** creates a full pathname by prepending the name of the current directory. UUCP maintains the full pathname as a pointer to the actual file. It does *not* copy the file into the spool directory before transmission. When contact is made with the remote system, UUCP then tries to access the file. The file must still exist at the time of transfer. (UUCP must also have permissions to read the file in that directory.)

Let's consider a scenario where you enter the command to transfer a file to another system. When UUCP tries to contact the remote system, the line is busy and it must try again at a later time. Meanwhile, thinking that you have transferred the file and no longer need it on your system, you delete the file. When UUCP finally gets through to the remote system, it cannot find the file that you specified and the request fails.

One way to get around such a problem is to use the -C option with **uucp**. It will actually copy the file to the spool directory (*/usr/spool/uucp*) instead of just storing a pointer to its location.

If you don't supply the pathname for a remote file, the source pathname will be used. This is probably not what you want.

```
% pwd
/work/jungle
% uucp book calif
%
```

The pathnames submitted to UUCP are:

```
/work/jungle/book  calif/work/jungle
```

UUCP will try to place the file *book* on the remote system in a directory */work/jungle*. If that directory does not exist, or you do not have permission to access that directory, the transfer will fail.

Referring to Parent Directory
Version 2

In Version 2, you cannot use the shorthand ".." to refer to the parent directory, as shown below.

```
% ls ../tbl.example
  ../tbl.example
% uucp ../tbl.example calif~/alice

permission denied /usr/fred/book/../tbl.example
uucp failed partially: 1 error
```

C Shell and Bourne Shell Examples

Let's look at a series of examples that illustrate how UUCP and the shell expand pathnames. It will also help to contrast differences in the use of UUCP in the C shell and the Bourne shell. In these examples, a dollar sign ($) prompt is used for commands submitted to the Bourne shell and a percent sign (%) is used for the C shell.

In these examples, we are copying files from *newton* to *calif*.

```
$ pwd
  /usr/fred/book
$ uucp chap1 calif!~/alice
$ csh
% uucp chap1 calif\!~/alice
```

Other than escaping the exclamation mark in the C shell, the two command lines are identical and achieve the same result. The UUCP request that's sent to the other system contains the following source and destination pathnames:

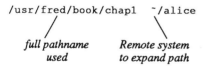

```
/usr/fred/book/chap1    ~/alice
```

full pathname used   *Remote system to expand path*

UUCP expands the relative pathname of the local source file and the tilde is not expanded in the destination pathname by **uucp** on the local system. The destination pathname will be submitted to the remote system for expansion. Additionally, the C shell did not expand the tilde; this character has special meaning only when it appears at the beginning of a pathname. Look at the following example for the C shell:

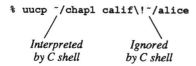

```
% uucp ~/chap1 calif\!~/alice
```

Interpreted by C shell   *Ignored by C shell*

The first tilde is expanded by the C shell into the pathname of the user's home directory. The second tilde, embedded in a pathname, is not expanded. The request that is submitted is:

```
/usr/fred/chapl    ~/alice
          /
  user's login directory
```

The Bourne shell ignores the tilde and thus the **uucp** command gets a chance to expand it into the pathname of the public directory.

```
$ uucp ~/chapl calif!~/alice
       /
    Expanded
    to PUBDIR
```

So the request that is submitted, provided that the source file exists, contains the following source and destination pathnames:

```
/usr/spool/uucppublic/chapl    ~/alice
```

Now let's look at some examples that use metacharacters to send or retrieve a group of files. We want to copy all filenames prefixed with "ch" in */usr/mary* on *calif* to a user subdirectory off the public directory on the local system. On the system *newton*, we enter:

```
$ uucp calif!~/mary/ch* ~/fred/
                     |
        metacharacter expanded
          by shell on calif
```

On the *newton* system, the destination pathname is expanded:

```
calif!~/mary/ch* /usr/spool/uucppublic/fred/
```

It is sent to *calif* where it expands the source pathname:

```
/usr/spool/uucppublic/mary/ch*
```

Let's consider the above example in the C shell. If we used the following source pathname in a **uucp** command:

```
calif\!~/mary/ch*
```

the following error message is displayed:

```
calif!~/mary/: No such file or directory
```

Placing the asterisk inside quotes or preceding it with a backslash will protect it from being interpreted by the shell. Likewise, the tilde in the destination pathname will be expanded to the user's login directory, not the public directory. Placing the tilde in quotes will make sure that **uucp** interprets it. In the C shell, the above example should be entered as follows:

```
% uucp calif\!~/mary/ch\* \~/fred
```

Beyond the PUBDIR

You are not restricted to the PUBDIR when sending remote files. It is possible to send a file to a specified remote directory. However, as we stressed at the beginning of this chapter, you may have trouble accessing that directory. Each remote system can limit file transfers to certain directories. Even when access is not specifically limited by the system administrator, file access modes on a remote system may keep you from completing a file transfer.

Remote Access Denied

If you try to transfer a file to a non-public directory, chances are that the request will fail. For instance, if you were on *calif* and tried to send a file to *newton*:

```
% uucp notes newton\!/usr/fred
```

You might eventually get back a mail message that reads:

```
From uucp Wed May 20 23:32:28 1987
Received: by calif.UUCP (4.12/4.7)
        id AA14904; Wed, 20 May 87 23:32:27 edt
Date: Wed, 20 May 87 23:32:27 edt
From: uucp (0000-uucp(0000))
Apparently-To: dale
Status: R
```

```
file /usr/fred/notes, system newton
remote access to path/file denied
```

/

status message

It informs you that a file transfer did not succeed because it could not access the directory */usr/fred*. When you are denied access to a file or directory, it can be either that the administrator has specifically denied that access to your system, or that the normal permissions of directories and files on the remote system have kept you out.

The administrator of a system can place restrictions or grant access to the various non-public directories on that system. This is done mainly to preserve the integrity and security of the local file system. The administrator specifies access privileges and restrictions in a UUCP configuration file (named *USERFILE* in Version 2; *Permissions* in BNU).

Access can be set for each system, but not for users of that system. In other words, all file transfers with a particular system are governed by this set of restrictions. All users on that system are treated alike.

For instance, the administrator can specify that **all** file transfers take place in PUBDIR. No amount of fiddling with file permissions can override this protection. The BNU administrator can set READ or NOREAD and WRITE or NOWRITE access for specific directories on the system. The actual file permissions of that file or directory can further restrict access; however, they cannot override UUCP security.

If you want to transfer to a non-public directory, the first thing you should do is ask the administrator if it is permitted.

File Permissions for File Transfer

If you are permitted to transfer outside the public directory, then you have to worry about file permissions. This is the same worry you have if you try to copy files from one place to another on your own file system. You must have read permissions for any file that you copy. You must have search (execute) permissions in any directory containing the file and all directories leading to it. You also need write permissions in any directory where you are going to copy a file.

There's one twist, though: UUCP is not you. That is, you might be permitted to copy from the remote directory or write into it, but the file transfer is conducted by UUCP working on its own. UUCP runs on the remote system as a user named *uucp* with the group *bin* or *other*. Processes running as *uucp* are governed by "other" permissions. It doesn't matter what "your" permissions are.

To view the file permissions for a given file, list that file's directory with the -l option. The permissions for each file are listed at the left of the screen.

```
% ls -l title
-rw-rw-rw-   1 fred      doc     1369 Dec 14 12:51 title
```

This unprotected file, named *title*, has read and write privileges for owner, group and others (0666). Earlier, we saw that a local file must be readable by others so that UUCP can access it. The same is true when retrieving a remote file.

If a remote file has read permissions only for the owner of the file and its group, you will not be able to access that file. In order to copy a file to or from a remote filesystem, the following rules should be observed:

- The file to be copied is readable by all (so that UUCP can read it at the time of transfer).
- The directories to which the file belongs must be readable and searchable by all (again, so that UUCP can access the file).
- The directory where the copy will be sent (either on the local or remote system) must be readable, writable, and searchable by all.

For example, to copy a local file called */usr/fred/plans* from *newton* to *calif*, the directories */usr* and */usr/fred* must have read/execute permissions for all.

Checking file permissions each time you copy or modify a local or remote file seems like a severe restriction of UUCP. Not only do local users have to tussle with the local file permissions, they also have to contend with remote file access modes. You have no way of knowing if a remote directory has the proper permissions for a successful file transfer unless you actually copy a file and get a message that the copy failed. For this reason, unless you know that file access and permissions have been worked out between the systems on your network, it is often easier to use the PUBDIR. In fact, many systems are so heavily restricted that only transfers to and from PUBDIR are allowed.

If you leave your files and directories unprotected in order to make file transfer easier, note that the potential for overwriting these files exists, and giving "all others" open access might be a decision you regret.

Sending Protected Files

In Version 2, the reason that the source file needs to be readable by all is that UUCP maintains only a pointer to the original file. When the transfer actually takes place, UUCP has to go back and get the file. If the file's permissions are owner access only, then *uucp* cannot read it to make a copy.

If a file is protected, and you don't want to change the permissions of the original file, you can use the -C option to copy the file to the spool directory.

In the Basic Networking Utilities, if a protected file is owned by the user, or in protected directories owned by the user, **uucp** will automatically invoke the -C option to copy the file to the spool directory. The copy will be owned by *uucp*.

If the user is *root*, the rules described above still apply: directories must be searchable by other and files must be readable by other.

Copying to a Remote User's Login Directory

Usually, when you send a file to a remote system, you want to send it to a specific person (i.e., to their login directory). UUCP has a special notation to refer to the login directory: the tilde (˜) character. The shorthand

    ˜user

automatically expands to the user's login directory. To send a file to a user on another system, all you need to know is the user ID. For example:

```
% uucp test calif\!˜mary
%
```

copies a local file called *test* in your present working directory to the login directory of user *mary* on system *calif*. Note that the UNIX file permissions mentioned earlier apply to both files.

Determining the Status of a File Transfer

When you enter a **uucp** command, you create a request that is queued for processing by the UUCP facility. Your request might not produce immediate results. It takes time for your system to connect with a remote system and to send the file.

If the connection to the remote system is over a telephone link, UUCP must first find a *device* (the modem) on which it can call out, then it must dial the number and make the phone connection to the remote modem. When the two modems are connected, the computers must go through a log in procedure. Only when the log in procedure is complete does your system start to send the actual file.

All of these connecting steps are performed by the UUCP daemon program **uucico**, and depending upon schedules set up by your system administrator, they might not even be started for hours to come. When you enter the **uucp** command, its function is to send two files to be spooled for **uucico**: a work file with instructions for the transfer, and (optionally) a data file that is a copy of the file to be sent. Once it has performed these tasks, the **uucp** program has done its job and is no longer active. If there is something wrong with the way you entered the **uucp** command itself (for example, if you forgot to enter a source or destination file), you will immediately receive an error message.

At each step of a file transfer, UUCP sends status messages to a log file. UUCP has several programs for tracking the progress of a transfer. In Chapter 4, *Checking on UUCP Requests*, we'll look at tracking UUCP requests by reading these status messages, and discuss what to do if the transfer has failed. In this chapter, we'll show you how to determine simply if a request is queued or completed, and how to kill a request that's waiting in the queue. Unfortunately, the command (or option) to perform these tasks differs in Version 2 and the Basic Networking Utilities.

"Is My Request on the Queue?"

Once you have created a UUCP job request, and put it on the spool queue, you might want to know when the job finishes or if it is still waiting to be processed. You can use the **uustat** command to get this information. You can also use it to kill a job that has not yet been processed.

A new version of **uustat** is shipped with the Basic Networking Utilities. The original **uustat**, shipped with Version 2, is more limited and displays different reports. (The **uustat** command is presented fully in Chapter 4, *Checking on UUCP Requests*.) Berkeley 4.3 supports yet another program called **uuq**.

---

uustat   *Version 2*

---

uustat alone, without any arguments, returns the status of all UUCP requests given by the current user. A job status is in either of two states: JOB DELETED, or JOB IS QUEUED. If a job is finished **uustat** gives a brief message such as COPY FINISHED, then JOB DELETED. If a job failed for some reason, **uustat** gives a brief error message, then JOB DELETED. If a job is still spooled and waiting to be completed, then **uustat** reports JOB IS QUEUED.

The report contains one line for each job with the most recent job at the top of the list.

```
% uustat
5616 fred waltham ... JOB IS QUEUED
5441 fred waltham ... COPY FINISHED, JOB DELETED
```

We'll look at what each of these fields mean in Chapter 4. The last field need only concern us now. It contains the *status* message, telling you that the job is still waiting in the queue or that it has been processed.

---

uustat   *BNU*

---

uustat alone, without any arguments, lists the current requests in the queue for the user. The report contains one line for each job with the most recent job at the top of the list.

```
newtonN5f76  05/20-23:38 S newton  bud 187 /ul/bud/chapl
```

We'll look at what these fields mean in Chapter 4. For now, it's sufficient to know that if the **uustat** report shows anything, then you have requests still waiting in the queue. When they no longer appear in the report, the request has been carried out.

uulog

There is no **uustat** command in Berkeley UNIX. You can use the **uulog** command to determine the status of a request. However, instead of getting one line per job, you will get a series of status messages for each job.

The **uulog** command takes an option **-u** followed by a user's id.

```
% uulog -ufred
mary newton (5/21-0:38-14993) QUE'D (C.newtonnDo81)
              .
              .
              .
mary newton (5/21-0:42-14993) OK (conversation complete)
```

Look for a status message that says "QUE'D". It will be followed by other messages which occur when the request was carried out. (We'll look at these messages in Chapter 4.) If you see a status message that says "OK", it means that the request was carried out. It doesn't necessarily mean that the transfer was successful, however.

Identifying a Job by Job Number

If you only want to follow the progress of a specific transfer job with **uustat**, you need to know the transfer's job number. To receive the job number of a transfer when you issue a **uucp** command, use the **-j** option, as in the following example:

```
% uucp -j plans calif\!/usr/mary/plans
Job 5378
%
```

To receive a report from **uustat** on that specific job, use the **-j***job#* option:

```
% uustat -j5378
5378 alice calif ... JOB IS QUEUED
```

If you forget to use the **-j** option when you issue a **uucp** command, you can invoke **uustat**, identify your job by your user ID, the system ID or the time it was sent, and copy down its job number from there.

Some Berkeley versions apparently do not support a **-j** option for the UUCP command. The BSD 4.2 documentation says that the job number is displayed when the command is accepted; however, that was not true on the system we tested (a Pyramid).

In Version 2, the job number is indeed a number; however, in BNU, a shortened system name serves as a prefix to a sequence of letters and numbers. A sample job ID from a BNU system might be **califN7283**. Be sure to use the entire job ID, not just the last four digits.

In Version 2, if the environment variable **JOBNO** is set to **ON**, the job number is automatically displayed when you issue the **uucp** command. When this variable is set, the **-j** option suppresses the job number message.

Killing a File Transfer Request

Sometimes you might change your mind about a UUCP transfer, or (even though you were warned not to) you might inadvertently send the same file twice. If the job is still queued, it is possible to kill your request using **uustat** and the **-k***job#* option. Only the *superuser* or the user who made the request can kill a job.

To kill the above job, you would enter:

```
% uustat -k5378
```

In BNU, you get a message saying that the job was killed. In Version 2, you don't get a message. To check that the job was killed, use **uustat** again:

```
% uustat
5378 tim calif ... JOB KILLED (COMPLETE)
%
```

If you try to kill a job that is already complete, you will get a message like **"job 5378 already complete - cannot kill."** You can only kill jobs that are still queued.

uuq -d

On Berkeley UNIX Systems, the **uuq** command with the **-d** option can be used to delete a job.

```
% uuq -d5378
```

5378 is the job number assigned to a specific UUCP request.

Make It Easy on Yourself

You can use shell scripts to customize the interface to the UUCP facility to your liking. Shell scripts can help to reduce the amount of input required to send a file to a remote system. For instance, if you frequently send files to a particular remote system, or to a particular user on that system, you can implement the command that you would normally type as a shell script.

For instance, if you were working on a project with another person on a remote system, you might be sending files back and forth.

```
% cat sendit
uucp -m -njohn $* newyork!~/john
```

This shell script invokes the **uucp** command with the following options: **-m** to notify the sender, **-n** to notify the recipient, *john*, and **-C** to copy the file to the spool directory before transmission. All the command line arguments are supplied as local filenames to the **uucp** command.

Use the **chmod** command to make this file executable.

```
% chmod +x sendit
```

Then you can use it. The following example sends the file *apple* to the remote system *newyork* and places it in the *john* subdirectory off the public directory.

```
% sendit apple
```

Once you have set up this command, you probably want to move it to a directory in your search path. Then you can execute this command in any directory on the system.

Both System V and Berkeley UNIX systems ship a number of shell scripts that interface with the UUCP programs. **uuto** and **uupick** are two examples that we looked at earlier in this chapter. You can modify these programs and create your own local version, if that makes it easier for you to use UUCP.

Another idea for a shell script is one that sends the same file to a list of remote systems.

```
for x in 'waltham newyork calif'
do
uucp -m $* $x!~/$LOGNAME/
done
```

This shell script sends any files specified on the command line to three different remote systems: *waltham*, *newyork*, and *calif*. It uses the environment variable LOGNAME to supply the user's id, which is used to place the files in a subdirectory of that name off the public directory.

Appendix A contains listings of several shell scripts that we use. You might enter these commands and try them out on your system. For example, the command **uuget** makes it easier to retrieve files from the public directory. Without arguments, **uuget** lists the files in the appropriate subdirectory of the public directory and asks you to take an action. You can move all or some files to the current working directory or do nothing.

```
% uuget
/usr/spool/uucppublic/fred:
status        takeme        takeme.too
Do you wish to move All files, Select files or
do Nothing:  Enter [A/S/N]s
Confirm files that you want to move: [Y/N/Q]
status :n
takeme :y
takeme.too :n
```

The result is that the file */usr/spool/uucppublic/fred/takeme* is copied into the current working directory. Consult Appendix A, *Useful Shell Scripts*, for more information on **uuget**.

Review of File Transfer

■ You must include the names of remote systems when identifying remote files. System names are followed by an exclamation point (! or \!).

■ File permissions limit the number of remote directories to which you can send or receive files.

■ The public directory (PUBDIR) is readable and writable by everyone. Its full path is */usr/spool/uucppublic*.

■ The **uuto** command copies files to a remote PUBDIR.

■ The **uupick** command picks up remote files in your PUBDIR sent to you by **uuto**.

■ The **uucp** command copies files to or from a remote PUBDIR or other directories as permitted.

■ In a **uucp** pathname, the tilde character followed by a slash (˜/) is an abbreviation for the pathname */usr/spool/uucppublic*.

■ In a **uucp** pathname, the tilde character followed by a user id (˜*user*) refers to a user's login directory.

■ When used with **uucp** or **uuto**, the **-m** option will notify the sender when a copy is complete. The **-n***rec* option will notify the recipient of a file sent with **uucp** (used by default with **uuto**).

■ The **uustat** command lets you know whether a job request is waiting in the queue, or if it has been processed.

3

Executing Remote Commands

Using the **uux** Command
Limitations of **uux**
Other Uses of **uux**

With the **uux** command, the UUCP networking facility can be used to execute commands on remote systems. However, there are broad restrictions on the commands that can be executed remotely. (The administrator on the remote system must give specific permission for remote users to access each command.)

These restrictions make **uux** less of a general-purpose program for a user. You are more likely to use the commands (**cu** or **tip**) to login on the remote system and execute commands (see Chapter 5, *Logging In on a Remote System*). A common use of **uux** is to access resources unique to a remote system, such as a printer. Thus, a system administrator might set up a local print command that invokes the **lp** or **lpr** command on a remote system.

Using the **uux** Command

The **uux** command is used to execute commands on a remote UNIX computer. When you invoke **uux** on the local system, you supply the name of the remote system and the command that you to want to be executed there. It causes a UUCP request to be queued up for the remote system. Once the request has succeeded or failed, you will be notified by **mail**.

For security reasons, **uux** is restricted to executing the commands that the remote system administrator has determined are safe for execution on that system. A typical installation might allow only the **rmail** and **rnews** commands for sending mail and news. Ask your system administrator for a list of commands that can be executed on the remote systems.

To show the use of **uux**, we're going to use a variety of printing commands. We'll assume that the remote system *waltham* permits these commands to be executed.

The first remote command that we execute is a standard System V command **enable**. We'll use it to make sure that the laser printer is enabled on the remote system.

```
% uux waltham\!enable laser
```
System   Command

This command will be sent to *waltham* and executed there. When you execute a remote command, UUCP will automatically send you mail that reports the status of the command.

```
From uucp Mon May 18 14:25 EDT 1987
>From uucp Mon May 18 14:40 EDT 1987 remote from waltham
Status: R

uuxqt cmd (enable laser) status (exit 0, signal 0)
```

uux In A Nutshell

---

uux [*options*] *command-string*

Execute a command on a remote UNIX system.

options

-      use standard input.

-a *user*
     notify *user* upon completion.

-b   print the standard input when the exit status indicates an error.

-c   do not copy files to the spool directory.

-C   copy files to the spool directory.

-g *c/n*
     set priority of transfer. If *c* is a "low" character such as "a" or "b", the job will be transferred before other jobs waiting to be sent. This also applies to *n* where *n* is a "low" number.

-j   print the **uucp** job number.

-l   (Berkeley only) make a link from the original file to the spool directory.

-L   (Berkeley only) start up **uucico**.

-n   inhibit *mail* notification.

-p   use standard input.

-r   queue the job but do not start communication program (**uucico**).

-s *file*
     send transfer status to *file* (a full pathname).

-x *n*
     specify the level of debugging output desired to be *n*, $0 \le n \le 9$. Higher numbers give more output.

A zero exit status means that the command has been executed successfully on the remote system. (At least on our system, we have not found the exit status to be entirely reliable.)

Local and Remote Files

The next step will be to send a file to the remote system. Again, let's assume that the remote system *waltham* permits the **lp** command to be executed by the local system *newton*.

This command will collect the file *printfile* from the local system, copy it to the remote system, and invoke **lp** there to print it.

```
% uux waltham\!lp -dlaser \!printfile
```

local file

The exclamation mark represents the local system. You could also specify the local system explicitly *(newton\!)*. Without the exclamation mark, UUCP will expect to find that file on the remote system.

UUCP has its own execution directory for running commands. It copies any files that it needs into this directory. If the file were interpreted as belonging to the remote system, and no pathname were supplied, UUCP would expect to find *printfile* in its own execution directory and the command would fail. The following request supplies the full pathname of file on the remote system.

```
% uux waltham\!lp /work/fred/printfile
```

path of file on waltham

You can also specify remote files on other systems.

```
% uux waltham\!lp calif!/work/fred/printfile
```

path of file on calif

UUCP is smart enough to use **uucp** to collect the file from the remote system, (providing it has permissions to access it) and copying into its execution directory before executing the **lp** command.

uux takes several optional arguments. A minus (-) option or (**-p**) tells **uux** to read from standard input and use it as the standard input of the command to be executed. For example:

```
% cat printfile | uux - waltham\!lp
%
```

tells **uux** to take input from the **cat** command and then supply it as standard input for the program **lp** to be executed on remote system *waltham*.

Use of Special Characters

The command string can consist of one or more commands allowed by the remote system, and can include special characters. Table 3-1 shows the special characters and operators that are and are not acceptable.

Table 3-1: Special Characters

Valid	Invalid
<	<<
>	>>
;	*
|	[ ]
	?

If used in a command string, special characters must be enclosed in a pair of double quotes. Alternatively, the whole command string, including the system name, must be enclosed in a pair of double quotes.

Suppose you are logged into system *newton* and you want to find out who is logged into system *waltham*. You can use the **uux** command and enter:

```
% uux "waltham\!who > newton\!~john/who.waltham"
%
```

The command string in this example consists of two commands. First, **uux** causes the **who** command to be invoked on *waltham*. Next, **uux** accumulates the output in a temporary file before using **uucp** to transfer the output back to the login directory of user *john* on system *newton*. This, of course, assumes that the **who** command can be executed on *waltham*.

You can also execute several commands on a remote system by using them in a pipe. However, all commands on the pipe must execute on the *same* system and only the first command in the pipeline must contain a system name. For example, the results of the **who** command above may also be piped to **rmail** (a restricted form of **mail**) and written as:

```
% uux "waltham\!who | rmail (newton\!john)"
%
```

The parentheses around *newton\!john* tell **uux** to interpret it as an argument to **rmail** and not as an input file. The **uux** command executes **who** on system *waltham* and pipes the output to **rmail**.

uucp normally notifies you if the requested command cannot be executed.

```
From uucp Thu May 14 18:15 EDT 1987
>From uucp Thu May 14 18:13 EDT 1987 remote from calif
Status: RO

uuxqt cmd (whodo ) status (DENIED)
```

The response comes by remote mail from the remote machine. If you do not want to be notified, use the **-n** option. You can also direct the message to a file with the **-m**file option. If *file* is omitted, you will receive mail when the copy is complete. For example:

```
% uux -m "waltham\!who > newton\!~john/who.waltham"
%
```

notifies you (*john*) when the command is executed.

Limitations of uux

The number and complexity of operations you can perform on a remote system are limited by the commands allowed by the remote system administrator. The administrator can make available commands to all remote systems or a specified few. The **rmail** program is the only command that is enabled by default (and is used to send you back messages that your remote command has failed).

Apart from security restrictions, there are some other intrinsic limits.

- You can't run a command interactively. As a rule of thumb, only a program that can run in the background without user intervention can be executed remotely.

- Standard output, unless redirected to a file or piped to a command, is normally lost.

- When redirecting output to a file, the file should be located in the public directory.

- A remote command is executed by the user "uucp" (not you). Processes created as a result of a remote command will belong to *uucp* and files are owned by *uucp*.

Other Uses of **uux**

You can perform more sophisticated operations, like sending messages to all users on the network or printing files from many systems, using **uux**.

Consider an environment consisting of several systems and a single printer shared among these systems. You can write a shell script to do remote spooling for those systems that are not directly connected to the printer. For example, from *newton*, you might include the following lines in a script to invoke the **troff** program (for formatting files) on a remote system called *waltham*, even though the files reside locally.

```
:troff a list of files and pipe to a printer
options=""
files=""
while [ "$#" != "0" ]
do
  case $1 in
      -*) options="$options $1";;
      *) if [ -f $1 ]; then
            files="$files $1"
         else echo "$1: cannot open"; exit
         fi;;
  esac
  shift
```

```
if [ -n "$files" -o ! -t 0 ]
  then cat $files |
  uux - "waltham!ditroff $options | lp"
fi
```

In order for this script to work, the commands **ditroff** and **lp** must be allowed on the remote system.

Review of Remote Command Execution

■ The remote system must be set up to allow you to execute the command.

■ To execute a command on the remote system, use:

uux [*option*] sys\!command

■ To send a local file in a remote command, prepend an exclamation mark to the pathname.

■ Use **-** or **-p** to instruct **uux** to take standard input as input to the remote command.

4

Checking on UUCP Requests

Using the **uustat** Command
Using the **uulog** Command
Checking the Logfiles Directly
Reading Status Messages

No sooner do you execute a UUCP command than you start worrying if your request will succeed. This chapter is about tracking your request, and what to do if it has failed.

Perhaps, if you have a reliable UUCP expert nearby, you might not want to bother learning more about UUCP (when you can bother him or her). It certainly isn't necessary to know what goes on behind the scenes to use the UUCP commands. But it has been our experience that you need to know more about UUCP if you are going to determine what went wrong with a UUCP request. (And things do go wrong.)

The new version of UUCP (BNU) is much better at sending mail messages to the user regarding failed requests. If you don't mind waiting for the mail, this can save you a lot of time tracking down your request. The mail messages we've seen are quite informative and some recommend an appropriate action.

We'll start off this chapter by looking at several UUCP programs that allow you to follow the progress of a UUCP transfer or remote command execution. **uustat** and **uulog** can be used to determine how far along a job is, and ultimately, whether it has succeeded or failed. **uustat** gives you a one-line summary for each job; **uulog** presents each of the status messages logged by a UUCP job. Then we'll look at the status messages that these commands display and what they mean. We'll examine the various stages of a UUCP request, and the related messages that are produced and whether or not they indicate a problem situation.

Should you want to learn more about UUCP, you might want to read the companion handbook, *Managing UUCP and Usenet*, which presents the installation and configuration process. In this book, Appendix B, *The Spool Directory*, is adapted from that book and is a guide to the directory (*/usr/spool/uucp*) where UUCP does its business. We will refer to it several times in this chapter.

Using the **uustat** Command

Use the **uustat** command to find out whether a job is finished or still waiting in the queue. **uustat** can also be used to remove any UUCP request from the queue.

The version of **uustat** that is shipped with the Basic Networking Utilities differs from the original **uustat**, shipped with Version 2. As shown in Chapter 2, *File Transfer*, the older version of **uustat** tells you the job status, usually going back a few days. A job status is in either of two states: JOB DELETED, or JOB IS QUEUED.

uustat In A Nutshell

uustat [*options*]

Provide information about **uucp** requests. This command can also be used to cancel **uucp** requests. Only **-u** and **-s** options can be used in combination with other options.

options

-a   report all queued jobs.

-k*jobn*
     kill request *jobn*.

-m   report accessibility of other systems.

-p   execute a "ps -flp" on the active communications processes.

-q   report the number of jobs queued for all systems.

-r*jobn*
     touch the files associated with *jobn*.

-s*system*
     report the status of jobs for *system*.

-u*user*
     report the status of jobs for *user*.

-o*hour*
     report status of **uucp** requests older than *hour*.<Xenix>

-y*hour*
     report status of **uucp** requests younger than *hour*.<Xenix>

Note: In Version 2, **uustat** without arguments returns the status of all UUCP requests given by the current user. A job status is in either of two states: JOB DELETED, or JOB IS QUEUED. The **-a**, **-q** and **-p** options are not available in this version.

In BNU, **uustat** without arguments lists jobs for the user that are still in the queue.

```
% uustat
5616 fred waltham 05/19-09:56 05/19-09:56 JOB IS QUEUED
5563 fred waltham 05/14-17:42 05/14-17:42 COPY FINISHED,
   JOB DELETED
5562 fred waltham 05/14-17:07 05/14-17:08 COPY FINISHED,
   JOB DELETED
```

```
5496 fred waltham 05/14-10:46 05/14-10:47 COPY FINISHED,
     JOB DELETED
5478 fred waltham 05/13-18:18 05/13-18:19 COPY FINISHED,
     JOB DELETED
5441 fred waltham 05/12-16:50 05/12-16:51 COPY FINISHED...
```

job#	*user*	*system*	*command-time*	*status-time*	*status*

job# is a number assigned by UUCP to the request. *user* is the userid of the person (*fred*) who initiated the transfer. *system* is the remote system name and *command-time* tells the date and time when the command was invoked. *status-time* gives the time of the given *status* message.

In this version, the report does not show the status of remote command executions. (Use **uulog** instead.)

In the BNU version of **uustat**, you get a list of jobs for the user that are in the queue. There is one line for each job with the most recent job at the top of the list.

```
newtonC701e 05/20-23:34 S newton bud 239 D.newto142f31b5
            05/20-23:35 S newton bud rmail charlie
newtonN5f76 05/20-23:38 S newton bud 187 /u1/bud/chap1
```

job ID	*requested*	*request*	*system*	*user*	*file size*	*file*

job# is a number assigned by UUCP to the request. *requested* is the date and time when the command was submitted. *Request* is a type of request; "S" is for sending and "R" is for receiving. *system* is the remote system name. *user* is the userid of the person (*fred*) who initiated the transfer. The *file size* in bytes and a pointer to the *source file* (or the name of a data (D.) file in the spool directory) are also listed. For remote command execution requests, these last two fields list the command and any arguments or files.

A slightly different report is displayed when the **-q** option is specified. It lists the jobs queued for each machine.

```
% uustat -q
calif     1C       05/20-23:41 CAN'T ACCESS DEVICE
newton    1C       05/20-23:48 Locked TALKING
texas     1C(1)    05/20-23:14 DIAL FAILED Retry: 0:15
```

If a status file exists for that machine, the report contains the system name, how many commands files are queued, the time of the last attempted contact with the remote system and the status resulting from that communication. (See Appendix B, *The Spool Directory*, to find out about status files.)

The status line for the remote system *texas* also lists in parentheses the number of days the request has been spooled. It also specifies the time (hours:minutes) until the retry period is up.

For a discussion of the status messages that appear in this report, see the section "Reading Status Messages" later in this chapter.

Jobs by User or by System Name

There are two particularly useful options you can use to classify UUCP jobs by user or by remote system. If you only want a report on jobs sent by another specific user (**uustat** without any options reports your jobs), use the **-u**_userid_ option. Use the **-s**_system_ option to list only those jobs that were sent to a specific remote system.

These options are available in both old and new versions of the **uustat** command. Here's the **-s** option shown with output from the older version:

```
% uustat -scalif
6220   fred calif 10/18-09:36 10/18-09:36 COPY FINISHED,
       JOB DELETED
6219 oscar calif 10/18-08:31 10/18-08:32 COPY FINISHED,
       JOB DELETED
6218 alice calif 10/18-08:25 10/18-08:25 COPY FINISHED,
       JOB DELETED
6217   fred calif 10/18-08:35 10/18-08:35 COPY FINISHED...
```

Here's the **-u** option shown with output from the BNU version of **uustat**:

```
% uustat -ufred
calif          05/20-23:41 (POLL)
natickC701e 05/20-23:44 S natick fred 239 D.att3142f31b5
            05/20-23:44 S natick fred  rmail fred
natickN701f 05/20-23:47 S natick fred 183 /u1/fred/chap1
newtonN5f76 05/20-23:38 S newton fred 187 /u1/fred/testfile
natickC701e 05/20-23:44 S natick fred 239 D.att3142f31b5
            05/20-23:44 S natick fred  rmail fred
natickN701f 05/20-23:47 S natick fred 183 /u1/fred/chap1
```

These two options can be combined with other options to select which listings appear in the report.

Checking Status of Remote Systems

The **-m** option to **uustat** will list the current status of communication with a remote system. You will get the status message for the last attempted contact with the remote machine.

In Version 2, you must supply the name of a specific remote machine as an argument with the **-m** option.

```
% uustat -mcalif
calif      05/21-16:49     CONVERSATION SUCCEEDED
```

You can specify **all** to get a complete listing of systems, which can be rather long.

In BNU, the **-m** option doesn't take an argument; by default it lists the status of all machines.

```
% uustat -m
calif      1C        05/19-03:41 CAN'T ACCESS DEVICE
natick     2C        05/20-23:41 SUCCESSFUL
newton     1C        05/20-23:48 Locked TALKING
newyork    1C        05/18-11:13 SUCCESSFUL
texas      1C(1)     05/20-23:16 DIAL FAILED Retry: 0:15
```

The format of this report is the same as for the **-q** option.

To specify the status of a particular machine, you can combine it with the **-s**system option:

```
% uustat -m -snewton
newton     1C        05/20-23:48  Locked TALKING
```

If BNU has trouble contacting a remote system, you will get a message in the mail, reading something like this:

```
From Root: Thu May 21 23:45 EDT 1987
   Subject: Warning from UUCP

We have been unable to contact machine
'calif' since you queued your job.

Job: newton!/ul/fred/testfile --> calif!~/fred (5/20)
```

```
The job will be deleted in several days if the
problem is not corrected. If you care to kill
the job, execute the following command:

    uustat -kcalif2N5f76

Sincerely,
newton!uucp
```

This is obviously a helpful message to receive. You should inform your system administrator of this problem.

uusnap (Berkeley)

On Berkeley UNIX systems, you can use the **uusnap** command to a show a "snapshot" of the UUCP network. For each system, **uusnap** displays a summary of jobs in the queue:

```
% uusnap
ora 2 Cmds  --- ---  LOGIN FAILED  Retry time 18 mins
ncr 2 Cmds  1 Data --- TALKING
```
site   *Work*   *Data*   *Xqts* *message*

where *site* is the name of the site with work, followed by the number of jobs for each type (see Appendix B, *The Spool Directory*, to find out about Work, Data and eXecute files), and *message* is the current status message. If UUCP has attempted to contact a remote system, and failed, the message also tell you how long until a retry.

Using the **uulog** Command

If you want a more detailed description of what is happening to your UUCP request, use the **uulog** command. **uulog** displays the status messages logged by UUCP programs for each job request. The status messages are listed in the sequence in which they occur with the most recent at the bottom of the report.

Just as with **uustat**, there are additional options available in the BNU version. In Version 2, **uulog** requires either the **-u** or **-s** option. You

uulog In A Nutshell

```
                              uulog [option]
       option

           -uuserid
                 Return file transfer status for a particular user.
                 (Not in BNU)

           -ssystem
                 Print status messages for file transfers to remote
                 system.

       BNU options

           -fsystem
                 Perform tail -f of log messages for system.

           -n    Display last n lines of log messages.

           -x    Check uuxqt file for given system or user.
```

can list status messages for any user with the **-u** option. (BNU dropped
this option.) The following example, showing Version 2 output, lists
status messages for Tom:

```
% uulog -utom
                          .
                          .
                          .
calif!tom (9/26-15:24:45)  (U,405,0) QUE'D (C.califnA8608)
calif!tom (9/26-15:25:12)  (C,407,0) REQUEST (S /tmp/phone
    /usr/mary tom)
calif!tom (9/25-15:25 27)  (C,407,1) REQUESTED (CY)
%
```

calif!tom indicates that user *tom* is sending a file to system *calif*. The
first line shows that *tom* has a file queued (QUE'D) to be sent to system
calif. The second line is a request for permission to start copying a file
called */tmp/phone* to the directory called */usr/mary*. The string
"REQUESTED (CY)" on the third line says that the send was successful. If not, the line would read "REQUESTED (CN)".

You can get information about **uucp** activity between two systems
using the **uulog -s**system command. The following example, showing
Version 2 output, lists the status messages for *calif*:

59

```
% uulog -scalif
calif!uucp (10/25-8:15:57)  (C,11593,0)  REQUESTED
    (S D.califXA5450 ...)
calif!uucp (10/15-8:16:47)  (C,11593,1)  COPY SUCCEEDED
calif!uucp (10/15-8:17:07)  (C,11593,2)  OK (conversation
    complete tty007 45)
                                  .
                                  .
                                  .
```

You can also combine the two options so that you can check all of a specific user's transfers to a specific system.

In BNU, **uulog** without any options lists the status messages for all systems. Because the list of log messages can be quite long, the BNU **uulog** command has added two options, *-n* which lists the last *n* lines of the report and **-f** which waits for current messages to arrive. Both of these options make use of the **tail** command and access log files in the spool directory. For instance, **-3** option with **-stexas** will list the last three status lines (most recent) for that system:

```
% uulog -3 -stexas
uucp texas (05/20-23:16:32,7363,0) CAN NOT CALL (SYSTEM
    STATUS)
uucp texas (05/20-23:22:14,7368,0) FAILED (LOGIN FAILED)
uucp texas (05/20-23:22:43,7368,0) CONN FAILED (DIAL
    FAILED)
```

Checking the Logfiles Directly

The spool directory (*/usr/lib/uucp*) also contains a number of logfiles that record the status messages for attempted transfers and remote executions.

As described in Appendix B, the spool directory in BNU has been reorganized. One of the important changes is that instead of a single LOG-FILE as in Version 2, there are logfiles in hidden subdirectories (they are hidden because they begin with a dot [.]).

Using Version 2, with its versions of **uustat** and **uulog**, we have come to rely on reading the LOGFILE directly. This doesn't seem necessary with BNU, as the same information is displayed by **uulog**.

LOGFILE

Version 2

In Version 2, the messages returned by **uustat** or **uulog** are not always as clear or complete as they could be. In particular, it is difficult to track **uux** requests with these commands. Therefore, in some cases, you will get more information by looking at */usr/spool/uucp/LOGFILE* itself. The LOGFILE contains all status messages for all UUCP jobs on your system. It may be a long file; if so use **tail** to look at the end:

```
% tail /usr/spool/uucp/LOGFILE
```

Identify your job by your user ID, by the system ID, or by the date and time you sent the request.

Reading Status Messages

Usually you can get all the information you need about a transfer from the **uustat** program, but if you learn from **uustat** that a job was deleted because of an error, or if a job seems to be queued for an abnormal amount of time, you can use **uulog** to find out what is going on. A complete list of the UUCP status messages is given in Appendix C, *Status Messages*.

It's important to understand that the status messages reported by **uulog** *are not necessarily error messages*. DO NOT repeat a UUCP command unless you are *sure* that the job has been deleted because of an error. Communicating over the phone line is not the best of environments for computers; modems on either end can be busy, wrong numbers can be dialed, and line fuzz can be interpreted as an error by either system. Consequently, most systems are set up to try UUCP requests over and over again. If you repeat a request, you will probably only end up spooling a second copy of the transfer, and tying up the line for that much more time.

For example, if you sent a request that went through fairly smoothly, the messages might read:

```
OK(DIAL number)
 TIMEOUT(LOGIN)
  SUCCEEDED(call to system)
   OK(startup)
    REQUEST(jobs)
     REQUESTED(jobs)
      COPY(SUCCEEDED)
       OK(conversation complete)
```

The TIMEOUT message merely meant that the remote system did not put up a login prompt in a given amount of time. Your system kept trying, and the second time the call SUCCEEDED. If you had repeated your request at that point, you would only have succeeded in sending a second copy of the transfer to the remote system.

It is best to read the status messages only *after* you have received the current status of the job from **uustat**. For example, if you sent a request at 8am, and received the following messages from **uulog** at 4pm, you might wonder if you should send the request again:

```
OK(DIAL number)
FAILED(call to system)
```

It could be that your system is set only to retry requests at the end of the day. If this were the case, **uustat** would read JOB IS QUEUED, and you would know not to send the request again. If your system has already tried to call as many times as it is set to call, and the call still failed, **uustat** would repost CALL FAILED, JOB DELETED. You could try the request again, or you might want to see your system administrator.

The following diagram follows a UUCP request through the daemon program **uucico** and lists the possible status messages you could receive along the way. Routine status messages are listed on the left; possible problem messages are listed on the right. Note that some messages appear in both columns because they depend upon the particular situation.

Now let's take an extended look at UUCP operations to learn how a file transfer request is handled and the possible problems and messages that may appear during that process.

During this discussion, we show various status messages without distinguishing which ones are given by Version 2 and which by BNU. We chose to emphasize the types of problems that can occur rather than the precise messages.

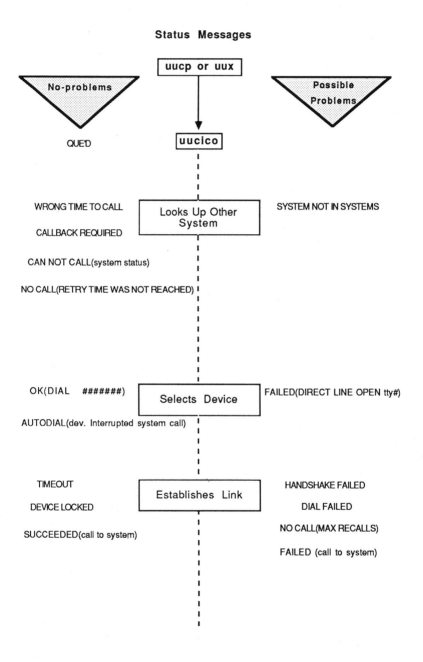

Status Messages

uucp or uux

No-problems

Possible Problems

QUE'D

uucico

WRONG TIME TO CALL

Looks Up Other System

SYSTEM NOT IN SYSTEMS

CALLBACK REQUIRED

CAN NOT CALL(system status)

NO CALL(RETRY TIME WAS NOT REACHED)

OK(DIAL   #######)

Selects Device

FAILED(DIRECT LINE OPEN tty#)

AUTODIAL(dev. Interrupted system call)

TIMEOUT

Establishes Link

HANDSHAKE FAILED

DEVICE LOCKED

DIAL FAILED

SUCCEEDED(call to system)

NO CALL(MAX RECALLS)

FAILED (call to system)

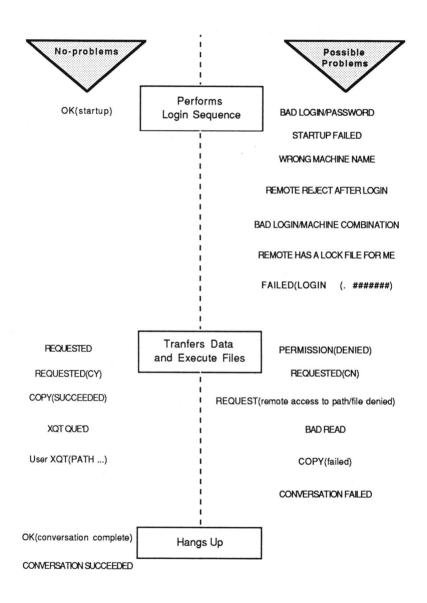

It's **uucico**'s Job

UUCP is a store and forward network. Requests for file transfers or remote execution of commands on another system are not executed immediately, but are spooled for execution when communication is established between the two systems. The **uucp** program itself doesn't copy files from system to system, nor does **uux** actually execute commands on a remote system.

When a user invokes either **uucp** or **uux**, three things happen:

- A work file containing information such as the name of the source file and the destination file, **uucp** or **uux** options, and the type of request (send, receive, or execute) is created in the directory */usr/spool/uucp*. If the user has invoked **uucp** with the -C option, a data file is also created, which contains an actual copy of the file to be transferred instead of just a pointer to it. Data files are also created whenever you send mail to someone on a remote system.

- The **uucico** program is invoked to actually make the transfer.

- A status file is created in the spool directory (or in a hidden subdirectory in BNU) that will contain the most recent status message.

When **uucico** is invoked, it scans the spool directory for work files, and attempts to contact other systems and execute the instructions in the work files. It creates lock files in the spool directory to make sure that no other copies of **uucico** try to call the other system at the same time.

However, the work files contain only a small part of the information **uucico** needs to know in order to make a transfer. They tell **uucico** what to do, but not when or how to do it. This information is contained in a set of files in the directory */usr/lib/uucp*, which it is the administrator's job to set up.

There are no status messages that result in this preliminary stage. (UUCP is creating the file or files that will contain these messages.) However, there is one type of message that might, but seldom does, appear at any time throughout a transfer: an *ASSERT* error. These are low-level operating system errors encountered by UUCP and should be referred to your system administrator for further investigation.

It Takes a *Systems* Approach

The most important of the configuration files is called *L.sys* in Version 2 UUCP, and *Systems* in BNU. It contains the list of systems known to the local system, together with instructions on how to reach each of them.

The entry for each system lists:

- The system name.
- Legal times to call (e.g. Any or Evening).
- The device to be used for making the connection (e.g. a modem or a direct line).
- The phone number of the remote system (if required).
- The login name and password UUCP should use to gain access to the remote system.

If you supply a remote system name that is not found in this file, you should get an error message immediately at your terminal. You may find this status message:

```
SYSTEM NOT IN Systems
```

Because it cannot identify the remote system by name, UUCP has not accepted your request. Use the **uuname** command to check the system name again.

The *L.sys* (*Systems*) file may explicitly restrict outgoing calls to a particular time. For instance, you may have requested a remote system that can only be dialed at night. In this case, the status message might read:

```
WRONG TIME TO CALL
```

UUCP will hold on to the request and keep trying until the time is right. This message might also be displayed if yours is a passive system and must wait to be polled by the remote system. The next message is similar, indicating that the local system, after notifying the remote system that it has work for it, will wait for the remote system to call it back:

```
CALLBACK REQUIRED
```

These messages indicate that arrangements have been made to restrict network usage, either for security or economic reasons. Needless to say, you must accept this arrangement or argue for it to be changed for all.

If UUCP has recently tried to call the remote system, and failed for some reason, it will not try to call again immediately. The status message might read:

```
CAN NOT CALL (SYSTEM STATUS)
NO CALL (RETRY TIME WAS NOT REACHED)
```

When **uucico** is unable to make the connection, it writes a message to the status file that contains the time last called and describes the status of the request. In Version 2, the status file is named *STST.system* and is found in the spool directory. In BNU, the status file is simply named for the called system, and is kept in a hidden subdirectory of the spool directory called *.Status*. The status file defers action on subsequent requests for that system.

As we have said before, if the first request fails to result in immediate action, a second request will have the same result; it does not cause UUCP to try again.

uucico will try again once a minimum retry period has elapsed. This minimum period is designed to keep UUCP from tying up the phone lines trying to call a remote system that is down. The default minimum retry period is 55 minutes in Version 2 UUCP.

BNU and Berkeley 4.3 use an "exponential backoff algorithm." That is, the retry period is shorter at first, and lengthens as the number of failures increases.

While you can be assured that UUCP will keep on trying to complete your request, there are some configuration and device problems that UUCP's dogged persistence will not resolve. If you can determine that the request has been tried several times and failed, then perhaps it's time to get your system administrator involved.

Left to Its Own *Devices*

Another file, *L-devices* (*Devices* in BNU), tells **uucico** which serial line the modem (or direct cable to another system) is attached to. The actual dialing instructions for the modem are either hardcoded into UUCP (in Version 2) or contained in the file *Dialers*.

If the transfer is able to proceed immediately, the message OK is written to the status file. But there are several reasons why the file transfer may not occur immediately.

Perhaps the modem or the outgoing phone line from your system is busy. You will see either message:

```
NO DEVICE AVAILABLE
CAN'T ACCESS DEVICE
```

If it succeeds in dialing the other system, but the other system doesn't answer, one of the following error messages will be displayed:

```
DIAL FAILED
FAILED (call to system)
```

These message could also indicate that there are problems with the entry in the *Devices* (*L-devices*) file.

When **uucico** contacts another system, it creates lock (LCK) files that prevent other attempts to contact the same system or use the same device. These messages are produced when **uucico** encounters them:

```
HANDSHAKE FAILED (LCK)
DEVICE LOCKED
```

The LCK files are normally deleted by UUCP once a job is finished and your request should succeed the next time it is tried. (Using Version 2, we have had on occasion to manually remove a LCK file that persisted long after a job was finished; see your administrator if you think this is necessary.)

There are also other reasons that these messages might appear, such as having the wrong device listed in the *Systems* or *Devices* files. Again, they require your system administrator's intervention.

Can We Talk?

When **uucico** is able to get through, it uses the last part of the line in the *L.sys* (*Systems*) file to log in to the remote system. This part of the line is often called the *chat script*, since it describes the conversation between the two systems. In this way, an automatic login can be performed. An obvious error message is produced by a failed login:

```
LOGIN FAILED
```

However, it isn't always obvious if a failed login is a fatal problem. It is if the chat script is at fault. But a bad connection or a slow machine can cause these problems, too, and perhaps the next attempt to login will succeed. Similarly, you might see the message TIMEOUT which simply means that the remote system did not respond within a set period of time.

If you think the problem is the chat script, see the system administrator or whoever set up the entry for the remote system in *Systems* (*L.sys*). The administrator can test it using the -x debugging option to **uucp** or **uucico**. See Chapter 4 on debugging in *Managing UUCP and Usenet* for more information.

Upon successful login, a **uucico** is fired up on the remote system. Two **uucico** programs, one on each system, will work in tandem to conduct the transfer. If there is a problem in initiating a conversation, you might see one of the following error messages:

```
STARTUP FAILED
REMOTE REJECT AFTER LOGIN
```

Next, the two systems introduce themselves. In most implementations of UUCP, both systems must be known to each other. That is, *newton* must have an *L.sys* entry for *newton*, and *newton* must have one for *newton*. Failure to verify the calling system might result in one of the following messages:

```
REMOTE DOES NOT KNOW ME
WRONG MACHINE NAME
BAD LOGIN/MACHINE COMBINATION
```

All of these messages indicate problems relating to the UUCP installation and configuration process and should be called to the attention of the system administrator.

It is possible that upon login that the other system was in the process of calling you. If UUCP finds a LCK file for the local system on the remote system, your request will fail temporarily, producing the following error message:

```
REMOTE HAS A LCK FILE FOR ME
```

A later retry should be successful.

Having a Conversation

After the preliminaries are out of the way, the actual transfer occurs. If all is going well, the status message is TALKING.

The **uucico** on the calling system controls the link, specifying the request to be performed (send, receive, or execute). The receiving system's **uucico** checks local permissions to see if the request can be performed, and if so, the transfer begins. If the transfer is not permitted, you might see either message (or receive it in the mail):

```
REMOTE ACCESS TO PATH/FILE DENIED
COPY(FAILED)
```

This is a problem you can handle yourself. Try resending the file to the public directory. See the section "Beyond the PUBDIR" in Chapter 2, *File Transfer*, for a discussion of proper file permissions for accessing non-public directories and files.

For a send request, the calling system sends packets of data; the receiving system sends back acknowledgements for each packet received. (Each packet is checksummed; packets that didn't come through correctly are re-sent.) For a receive request, the reverse is true. While the file is being received, it is stored in a temporary file in the target system's spool directory; once the transfer is complete, the target system's **uucico** copies it to the requested destination.

If any of the requests processed were for remote command execution (that is, **uux** requests), an execute file is created in the spool directory of the remote system.

During the transfer, several problems might occur. One is that the remote system might run of space, producing the following error message:

```
BAD READ
```

The communications link could fail (somebody flicked off the modem; pulled a cable; either system crashed; or a lightning strike). After such unexpected events, the mild message might be:

```
CONVERSATION FAILED
```

Don't worry, UUCP won't allow a partial job to be considered complete. It will resend the entire file or message after the retry period has elapsed.

Hanging Up

When the calling system's **uucico** is done with all of the requests it has queued for the remote system, it sends a hangup request. If the remote **uucico** has any business of its own to transact (including requests for files needed for remote command execution), it refuses the hangup, and the roles are reversed.

When nothing is left to be transferred in either direction, the two **uucicos** agree to hang up. If there was an execute request, another daemon called **uuxqt** is then fired up on the remote system to process the request. It reads the execute file in its spool directory, checks that it has permission to execute the requested command, and makes file transfer requests of its own if it needs additional files from the original system in order to carry out the command. If all went well, **uuxqt** finally does what the user asked.

A final message from a successful communication between two system is:

```
CONVERSATION SUCCEEDED
```

However, this message just refers to the exchange of requests and data between the two systems. It doesn't necessarily mean that your request achieved what you wanted on the remote system. An exchanged request might fail once the remote system tries to carry it out, for instance, when retrieving a file from that system or when executing a remote command.

5

Logging In on a Remote System
Remote Login With cu
Tilde Escape Sequences

The **cu** program is more general than UUCP, since it allows you to log in directly to a remote UNIX or non-UNIX system and execute commands interactively on that system. **cu** is useful if you regularly use more than one UNIX system or if you dial up non-UNIX systems such as on-line databases.

Before you can use **cu**, you need a valid login name and password to the remote system. If you don't already have a login on the remote system, contact the remote system administrator to request a login name and password that you can use on the remote system.

Berkeley UNIX systems supply a program called **tip** for remote login. (Some Berkeley systems also support **cu**.) **tip** is very similar to **cu**, and many regard it as a better program. We provide a Nutshell summary of **tip** in this chapter. Consult your system documentation for more information on **tip**.

Remote Login With cu

cu can be used to contact systems that are members of your UUCP network, or other systems, including non-UNIX systems. Like **UUCP, cu** can communicate over dial-up and hardwired connections. We assume that these physical connections have been made and tested by your system administrator. (This is also described in the companion handbook, *Managing UUCP and Usenet*.)

With **cu**, you can login to a remote system from your terminal on the local system. During this session, the local system acts transparently, transmitting input from your terminal to the remote system and receiving output from the remote system and displaying it on your terminal screen. It is just as though your terminal were directly connected to the remote system.

One difference you might notice is that the speed of transmission is typically slower, especially over phone lines, and thus system response might be delayed. Also, when communicating over phone lines, you will on occasion get a bad connection, one that causes a lot of garbage characters to appear on your screen. You might disconnect and dial in again to see if you get a better line.

Contacting a Remote System by Name

You can use the name of the remote system to establish a connection with another UNIX system on the UUCP network. (Some older versions of **cu** might not support the use of UUCP system names.) The names of remote system that you can contact can be listed with the **uuname** command. For example, to dial-in to system *calif*, you would enter:

```
% cu calif

Connected
login: boston
Password:

calif%
```

cu In A Nutshell

cu [*options*] *telno* | *dir* | *system*

Call up another UNIX system or a terminal via a direct line or a modem. A non-UNIX system can also be called. When a *system* is known to UUCP, the command "**cu** *system*" handles the connect options.

options

-a*acu*

specifies device name of ACU (automatic calling unit) device.

-d   print diagnostics of session.

-e   use even parity.

-l*line*

line is the name of the communications line device.

-h   emulates local echo and supports calls to other computer systems which expect terminals to be in half duplex mode.

-o   use odd parity.

-s*speed*

set the baud rate to *speed*.

-t   dial an ASCII terminal with auto answer set.

telno

the telephone number. Use = to wait for a secondary dial tone; - to get a brief pause.

system

call the *system* known to UUCP.

After entering the **cu** command, you should get the system response "**Connected**." This shows that a link between the local system and *calif* has been made. *calif* should then display the login prompt. Enter the login name and password for the remote system that were given to you. If these are correct, *calif* will give you some system messages and finally, the system prompt (*calif%*).

When you get the remote system prompt, you can start entering commands just as if you were on a terminal directly connected to it. See the section "Disconnecting from **cu**" below to learn how to end a remote login session.

cu accesses a UUCP configuration file, *L.sys* (*Systems*), to get the name of the remote system, the type of device used to make the connection and the phone number, if any. Because the system *calif* is set up on your UUCP network, you can use its name to contact it. This configuration file can also be used to identify other systems that are not UUCP sites. Thus, you can set up entries for public bulletin boards or non-UNIX systems that you wish to contact regularly. However, access to this UUCP configuration file is usually restricted so you should have the system administrator add this information for you. Thus, if get an entry for *bix* (Byte Magazine Information Exchange), you can call that bulletin board by entering:

```
% cu bix

Connected
```

If you use **tip**, the system configuration file is not the same as UUCP's. The program looks in files named */etc/remote* and */etc/phones*. Therefore, just because you can contact the remote system through UUCP doesn't necessarily mean you can use the system name for remote login with **tip**.

Specifying a Phone Number

If you want to call a system that is not on your UUCP network, you must specify the phone number of the remote system. On some systems, this can be as simple as:

```
% cu 19615555
connected
```

On other systems that have several call-out devices, you might need to specify the line or device with the -l*device* option.

```
% cu -ltty006 19615555
```

This instructs **cu** to dial out over serial line *tty006*.

If there is a direct connection to the remote system, you would only specify the line. Similarly, on some systems, you may use **cu** to connect to the modem or other communications device. Then you may have to "talk" to the modem directly. Instead of supplying the phone number on the command line, you will have to enter special commands, such as a **D**, instructing the modem that you want it to dial a number. Ask your system administrator to walk you through this procedure.

If you are making the connection yourself, you will have to make sure that the communications parameters of your system match those on the remote system.

By far, the most important communications parameter is the baud rate or the speed at which both systems agree to exchange data. (e.g., a 300 baud and a 1200 baud modem). You can specify the baud rate with the -s*speed* option. It can also be used to specify a device with that baud rate. If you don't specify the baud rate, **cu** will use the default setting for that serial port.

For example, the command below tells **cu** to use a modem with a line speed of 1200 baud in calling a remote modem with the phone number "9=1-6924435."

```
% cu -s1200 9=1-6924435
```

The equals sign (=) tells the dialer in the modem to wait for a dial tone (for example, to get an outside line) before dialing the rest of the digits. The dash (-) implies a one-second pause. Ask your system administrator if you are unsure about what line speed or device to specify, if any.

Problems Making the Connection

There are a variety of problems that might occur when you try to connect to a remote system. First, we'll look at those messages that you see instead of or before the **Connected** message appears on your screen.

If you supply an invalid system name or the wrong device name, the connection will fail and you will get the message:

```
Connect failed: Requested device/system name not known.
```

The most obvious problem is that there is not an entry under that system name in the UUCP configuration file *L.sys* (*Systems*). Verify the system name (using **uuname**); it is possible that you mistyped it.

If you identified a serial port, and got the above message, it may be that you just supplied the wrong line number. Or that the administrator changed the port for this type of connection since you last tried to make contact. It might also turn out that the line is not properly configured for use. Check with your administrator.

Before accessing the specified line or device, **cu** checks to make sure that UUCP is not currently using it. If the modem or the serial line is busy, then you might get the following message:

```
Connect failed: No Device Available
```

Wait and try again. If problems persist, see your system administrator. On Version 2 UUCP systems, a lock file (LCK..*system* or LCK..*line*) or a status file (STST.*system*) in the spool directory indicates that the system or device is being used by UUCP. Until these files are removed by UUCP, you cannot contact that system or use that port. If you think these files are not recent, see your system administrator about deleting them.

If you get the **Connected** message but no login prompt, press RETURN once or twice. Also try pressing the Break key.

If no login prompt appears, it is possible that when your modem called the remote system, their line was busy. You probably won't get a message. If you are near the modem and it has a speaker, you'll hear the busy signal; otherwise, after waiting a sufficient period of time, disconnect from **cu**. (See the section "Disconnecting from **cu**" below.)

If you are getting through to the other modem, but see no login prompt on your screen, ask the remote system administrator to check that there is a **getty** on the line at his end.

If you get through, but see garbage on your screen, either you have a horrible connection, or the communications settings on the two systems are not the same. This is a problem that your system administrator will have to work on.

There is also a debugging option (**-d**) that a knowledgeable user or administrator can use to locate other problems in establishing communications with another system.

Tilde Escape Sequences

cu runs as two processes: transmit and receive. Transmit reads from standard input and passes lines to the remote system. Receive reads data from the remote system and passes it to the local system. (**tip** also has transmit and receive processes.) Both processes filter out lines beginning with a tilde (˜) which **cu** then interprets as commands.

These commands, or *tilde escape sequences*, perform a variety of tasks. **cu**'s tilde escape sequences are listed in Appendix E. On some systems, when you enter the tilde, it will prompt you with the system name in brackets:

```
calif% ˜[newton]
```

Enter the command letter or word and press RETURN. Perhaps the most important of these is to end a remote login session (˜. or tilde-dot), as shown in the next section. Ahead, we'll look at some tilde escape sequences that allow you to move back and forth between the local system and the remote system.

Disconnecting from cu

To log out and disconnect a **cu** link, log out, then enter tilde-dot (˜.) sequence on a new line and press the RETURN key.

```
calif% logout
California Systems
login: ˜.
Disconnected
%
```

After entering this exit sequence, **cu** tells you that the remote system is disconnected. You remain logged into the (local) system and you will get the local system prompt (%).

Depending on how the dial-in line on the remote system is set up, disconnecting **cu** may or may not also log you out. Unless you know for sure that the remote system will log you out when you disconnect, you should first log out of the remote system before disconnecting.

tip In A Nutshell

---

tip [*option*] [*name/number*]

Establish connection to another machine. Remote machine may be identified by a recognizable *name*, or by a telephone *number*.

options

    -speed

        establish connection at baud rate *speed*.

---

tip Tilde Escapes In A Nutshell

˜.   disconnect from remote system (may not hang up).

˜c[*dir*]

    change directory to *dir* on local system.

˜!   escape to a shell on local system.

˜>   copy file from local to remote system.

˜<   copy file from remote to local system.

˜p*file*[*target*]

    send *file* to remote UNIX host.

˜t*file*[*target*]

    take *file* from a remote UNIX host.

˜| pipe output from remote command to local process.

˜$ pipe output from local command to remote process.

˜#   send a BREAK to remote system.

˜s   set a variable.

˜˜Z   stop **tip** (with job control only).

˜˜Y   stop only "local" **tip** process (with job control only).

˜?   print summary of tilde escapes.

Tilde-Tilde

If you log into a remote system (*calif*), and then use its **cu** program to contact yet another remote system (*japan*), you have two different **cu** programs running. You may need to move back and forth between three machines. For instance, if you logged out of *japan* by entering ˜., then you would end up on the local system, completely bypassing *calif*.

If you want the second machine (*calif*) to receive a tilde- dot escape sequence, enter tilde-tilde-dot. Thus, entering ˜˜. on *japan* would return you to *calif*.

Transferring Files With cu

cu provides a method for transferring small text files between UNIX systems that are not on the UUCP network. However, its file transfer capability lacks checksumming or spooling, so it is a less preferred way of transferring files when UUCP links are available. Your files may arrive garbled, or with pieces missing.

The **cu** commands for transferring files between UNIX systems are ˜%take and ˜%put. There's usually some degree of confusion about the direction of file transfer when you use these commands. Perhaps it will help to remember that the local system is your point of reference in file transfers. Thus, you *take* a file from the remote system and, in reverse, you *put* a file to the remote system.

Take From Remote

To copy a file from the remote system, you would *take* the file and copy it over to your system. The syntax is:

˜%take *from* [*to*]

˜%take is a tilde escape that you enter once you are logged on to the remote system. (Using **tip**, enter ˜%t.) *from* is the name of the remote system file and *to* is the name you want to give the file on your system. The new filename (*to*) is optional; **cu** uses the original name of the file if it is not given.

For example, to copy the file *test* from system *calif* and assign it the same filename on the local system:

```
calif% stty tabs
calif% ~%take test
stty -echo;mesg n;echo '~>':test;cat test;echo '~>';mesg y;
stty echo
~>:test
2 lines/85 characters
calif%
```

The **stty tabs** commands may need to be invoked before you use
~**%take** so that any tabs present in the file will not be expanded into
spaces when the file is transferred. When you issue the ~**%take** command, the system prints two control lines. The control lines form a
shell script that consists of commands that go to *calif* to transfer the file
called *test*. The last line tells you the number of lines and characters
transferred. This is printed out when the process is complete.

Let's see what the commands in the ~**%take** script mean. (Note that
you don't need to type this dialog. It is described in detail so you can
understand what is happening.)

Table 5-1: ~**%take** Script Commands

Command	Description
stty -echo	Do not echo back every character typed.
mesg n	Do not allow any messages sent to the user's termi-nal by other processes to interfere.
echo '~>':*test*	Send the string "~>:*test*" to the standard output of the remote system, where *test* is the name of the file to be copied. The notation "~>:*file*" echoed on the remote system diverts the output to a file on the local system.
cat *test*	Send the file called *test* to standard output.
echo '~>'	Send the string "~>" to the standard output of the remote system. This ends the output diversion.
mesg y	Allow messages to be sent to the user's terminal.

The **stty** and **mesg** commands perform "housekeeping tasks." The cru-
cial commands that perform the file transfer are **echo** and **cat**. (These
two commands should exist on the remote system). Thus, you can
write a shell script using the same syntax to perform additional tasks.
For example, you could create the following script that allows you to

copy multiple files from the remote system to your local system.

```
for x
do
      echo "~>:$x"
      cat $x
      echo "~>"
done
```

Assuming that you have saved this script on the remote system in a file called **takeit**, the command:

```
% takeit file1 file2
```

would "take" *file1* and then *file2*. The command:

```
% takeit *
```

would "take" all of the files in the current directory on the remote system.

˜**%take** does not work when you copy files from a non-UNIX system. However, since you already know what each command in the ˜**%take** script does, you can sometimes still write a script containing commands on the non-UNIX system that perform the same functions as **cat** and **echo**.

Put on Remote System

When you want to copy a file from the local system to another system, you are essentially *put*ting it on the other system. You would enter the command ˜**%put** while logged in to the remote system:

˜**%put** *from* [*to*]

˜**%put** is a tilde escape that you enter once you are logged on to the remote system. (Using **tip**, enter ˜**%p**.) *from* is the name of the local file and *to* is an optional name for the file on the remote system. For example, to copy a file called *plans* in your working directory on the local system to a file called *plans.new* on another system, you would enter:

```
calif% ~%put plans plans.new
stty -echo; cat - > plans.new; stty echo
12 lines; 184 characters
%
```

cu sends a control line for the file transfer and prints the number of lines and characters sent when the transfer is complete.

You can specify a full pathname as the *from* filename, but you should be sure to specify a *to* filename as well, since the ˜%put will fail if it includes the name of a directory that is not present on the other side.

For example, the command:

˜%put */usr/tim/test*

would fail if the directory */usr/tim* did not exist on the remote system. However,

˜%put */usr/tim/test test*

would work, since the *to* file will be created in the current directory on the remote system. The script will automatically be terminated when you disconnect **cu**.

Executing Commands Locally

When you are logged into a remote system using **cu**, you can execute any command on the remote system. You can also execute commands on the local system from the remote system without interrupting the connection.

You have already seen two of the tilde escape sequences, ˜%take and ˜%put, for transferring files. To run a command on the local system while logged into the other system, enter the command as:

˜!*command*

For example, if you are calling *calif* from *boston*, you can still find out who is logged in on *boston* using the **who** command, as in the following example:

```
calif% ˜!who
lamb       tty002      Oct 23   10:10
sue        tty003      Oct 23   10:04
dale       tty020      Oct 23   08:56
tim        tty005      Oct 23   13:13
!
calif%
```

Simply typing ¯! followed by a RETURN lets you escape to an interactive shell on the local system.

You can also send the output of a command to the remote system, while running it on the local system, by using:

¯$command

One possible use of this escape sequence is in copying a file from a local UNIX system to a remote non-UNIX system. For example, assume you are logged into a VAX/VMS system (called *mars*) using **cu**, and you would like to copy a text file called *test* from your UNIX directory. While on *mars*, you would enter:

```
mars$ create test.vms
mars$ ¯$cat test.UNIX
```

(The **create** command on the VAX is similar to the UNIX "cat >" for creating text files. The second line invokes the **cat** command on the local (UNIX) system, but the output of the command is sent to the remote system, where it is presumably captured in the file that was just created (*test.vms*). Typing CTRL-Z would close the file on the VAX.)

Changing Directories

If you try to change directories on the local system using the tilde shell escape (¯!), your command is submitted to a sub-shell and has no lasting effect. Use the sequence ¯% instead. Look at the following example:

```
calif%¯!pwd
¯[newton]!pwd
/work/nutshell/uucp
!
¯!cd /work/fred
¯[newton]!cd /work/fred
!
¯!pwd
¯[newton]!pwd
/work/nutshell/uucp
!
¯%cd /work/fred
¯[newton]%cd /work/fred
```

```
calif%~!pwd
~[newton]!pwd
/work/fred
!
```

The sequence **%cd** allows you to change the working directory on the
local system; this persists for your remote login session. Note that
when you disconnect from the remote system, you will return to the
local directory that you were in when you began **cu**.

tip Environment Variables

tip differs from **cu** in that it allows variables which control its opera-
tion to be set within its environment. Variables may be set during the
tip session with the ¯s escape sequence, or may be set automatically
upon entering **tip** by specifying options and their values in *.tiprc* in the
user's HOME directory. In *.tiprc*, the ¯s prefix should be omitted.

tip variables have boolean, numeric, string or character values. An
assignment should not have blanks in it. Numeric, string and character
values can be set by combining the variable with "=" and a value (e.g.,
¯s **ba=1200**), while boolean values are set just by naming them, or
unset by naming them with the "!" prefix (e.g., ¯s **!verb**).

All options can be displayed with the escape ¯s **all**.

Table 5-2: **tip** Environment Variables

tip Variable	Type	Description
beautify (be)	*bool*	Discard unprintable characters in session script.
baudrate (ba)	*num*	Baud rate for connection.
dialtimeout (dial)	*num*	Time before connection should be abandoned.
echocheck	*bool*	Wait for echo of last character transmitted during file transfer. Default is *off*.
eofread (eofr)	*str*	String signifying end of transfer during ¯< file transfer.

Table 5-2: tip Environment Variables *continued*

tip Variable	Type	Description
eofwrite (eofw)	*str*	String signifying end of transfer during ˜> file transfer.
eol	*str*	String signifying an end-of-line.
escape (es)	*char*	Escape character. Default is ˜.
exceptions (ex)	*str*	Characters which should not be discarded by beautification. Default is \t\n\f\b.
force (fo)	*char*	Character to force literal data transmission. Default is ˆP.
framesize (fr)	*num*	Amount (in bytes) of data to be written to buffer between writes in receiving files.
host (ho)	*str*	Name of host.
prompt (pr)	*char*	Character signifying end-of-line on remote host. Default is \n.
raise (ra)	*bool*	Map lower case letters to upper case on remote machine. Default is *off*.
raisechar (rc)	*char*	Character used to toggle upper case mapping mode. Default is ˆA.
record (rec)	*str*	Name of file in which session script is recorded. Default is *tip.record*.
script (sc)	*bool*	Record everything transmitted by remote system in script record file, except those affected by the **beautify** switch. Default is *off*.
tabexpand (tab)	*bool*	Expand tabs to spaces in file transfer (8 spaces each). Default is *off*.
verbose (verb)	*bool*	Print messages while dialing and during file transfer. Default is *on*.
SHELL	*str*	Name of shell for use by ˜! escape. Default is taken from the environment (usually **/bin/sh**).

Table 5-2: tip Environment Variables *continued*

tip Variable	Type	Description
HOME	*str*	Home directory for use by ˜c escape. Default is taken from the environment.

Making a Script of a **cu** Session

Sometimes (for example, when calling up an on-line database) you may want to create a script of an entire **cu** session. (This is also a way of capturing files from a non-UNIX system, since the files of interest can be typed to the screen, captured in the script, and broken out later with a text editor.)

Some versions of **cu** support an option to automatically create a script. Check your system's UNIX reference manual.

On systems which do not support this option, you can set the same result using either the **script** or **tee** commands. **script** simply keeps a record of all transactions at the terminal. Everything that appears on the screen is copied into a file, named **typescript** by default. For example:

```
% script
Script started, file is typescript
% cu ...
```

After terminating **cu**, type ^D to terminate the script.

tee is a "pipe splitting" utility. Output piped through **tee** is copied— one copy goes, as usual, to standard output, the other can be piped on to other programs or put into a file.

tee is not a generalized scripting utility, since it will only work with the output of a single command. However, in the case of **cu**, the entire dialogue with the remote system can be thought of as the standard output of a single **cu** command. The result is therefore the same as for **script**.

To make a transcript of a **cu** session with **tee**, type:

```
UNIX% cu ...  | tee scriptname
```

Review of Remote Login

To summarize this chapter:

■ Establish a link to a remote system with:

        cu *system*

or:

        cu -s*speed phone*

or:

        cu -s*speed* -l*line*

■ Copy a file from the remote system to the local system while on the remote system with:

        ˜**%take** *from* [*to*]

■ Copy a file from the local system to the remote system while on the remote system with:

        ˜**%put** *from* [*to*]

■ Execute a command on the local system, while on the remote system with:

        ˜**!***command*

■ Change the directory on the local system with:

        ˜**%cd**

■ Send the output of a command to the remote system, while running it on the local system with:

        ˜**$***command*

6

Extending the UUCP Network

Beyond the Local Network
The **mailx** Program
Transferring Binary Files
Forwarding Files
Transferring Multiple Files or Directory
   Hierarchies

In this chapter you will learn how to:

☐ Send mail and forward files to remote systems that are not on your local network.

☐ Use some of the time-saving features of **mailx** to make it easier to send mail.

☐ Transfer binary files through the mail.

Beyond the Local Network

It is probably clear to you by now that a UUCP connection is point-to-point and simply involves an agreement between two systems to exchange system names and other information. Unless the system administrators of the systems to which you are directly linked devise a way to announce your existence, others on the network are unaware of you and you of them.

Many local networks are indirectly tied to a larger network through Usenet. Even though Usenet is strictly-speaking the network of systems that agree to exchange news, it is a fairly safe bet that your system is connected to Usenet. You can send mail to anyone on any of the 6000-odd sites in the net. There are several different ways to "address" the mail, depending on what version of the Usenet software your system and the destination system is running.

Find Your Backbone

The most basic method, and one that you can always use, is to determine the complete path between your system and the system you want to reach.

This is not as difficult as it might seem, since the network includes a number of major sites, called *backbone sites*. A backbone site is a system that serves as a major mail exchange; it exchanges mail and sends and receives every nonlocal news item (see Chapter 6) with at least two other backbone sites.

You need to know only two things in order to reach anyone on the net: the path from your system to any one of the backbone sites, and the path from any one of the backbone sites to your destination. Putting the two together will give you a complete path to your destination.

UNIX users who make use of the net will often publish their "net address" — that is, the path from one of the major sites to their own system and login name. For example, in your reading, you might have come across some articles on UNIX where the authors give a path to their system in case you want to correspond with them. An address might be given as:

```
uunet!ism780c!phw5!pat
```

The first system in the net address is a backbone site or other well-known system. It is followed by one or more other system names, ending with the target system, and finally, the login ID of the user.

You might also see an address like this:

```
{ucbvax | usenix}!joe
```

This form signifies that *joe* can be reached either on (or through) *ucbvax* or *usenix*.

The second is written in a special format called *internet* format, which is recognized by some mail programs. It is often used to address mail to sites on Usenet which are not linked via UUCP.

Domain is an organizational or geographic subdivision. In the U.S., there are six top-level domains: com (commercial); edu (educational); mil (military); gov (government); net (networking organizations); and org (other organizations). In Europe, geographic domains are used— for example, UK for United Kingdom. Geographic domains are also coming into use in the U.S. You may also see a network, such as ARPA, UUCP, or BITNET used as a domain name, but this is not correct Internet format. *Subdomain* is usually an organization within the domain—for example, ora.com for O'Reilly and Associates or mit.edu for the Massachusetts Institute of Technology. However, there can be multiple levels of subdomains—for example, lcs.mit.edu is the Laboratory for Computer Science at MIT.

At any rate, once you have the address from a backbone site to a user you want to reach, you must figure out your path to one of the other backbone sites.

To derive a path to a backbone site, you need to find out if any of your immediate neighbors are gatewayed to it. Probably the simplest way to do this is to ask your system administrator. (If you are the system administrator, read on.)

For the sake of example, let's say that you're on system *waltham*, and that your path from the backbone site *decvax* is called *decvax!newton!waltham!john* . You want to send mail to *pat* whose address from the backbone site *ihnp4* is *ihnp4!phw5!pat*. To send mail to *pat*, you would enter:

```
% mail newton!decvax!uunet!ism780c!phw5!pat

Whew! I almost got lost typing your address.
What's up?
                        --John D. of newton
^D
%
```

You can assume that the two backbone sites *decvax* and *uunet* can reach each other. However, as user *john* noted above, network addresses can get to be unwieldy. For this reason, considerable effort has been put into developing some tools to make network addressing easier.

The *Pathalias* Program

Some systems have a database of net addresses that a program called **pathalias** uses to figure out the path to a remote system. On these systems, you can address mail directly to the target system, and the address gets expanded automatically to the appropriate pathname. (The database is posted monthly in the Usenet newsgroup *comp.mail.maps*. **Pathalias** is a public domain program made available over Usenet; it reads the database and generates a file containing paths from your system to every other system on the net. **Smail**, another public domain program that is used in place of **rmail**, reads the path data provided by **pathalias** and actually does the mail forwarding. Another program, **uuhosts**, can be used to maintain or query the database for path information.)

The **mailx** Program

The System V **mail** program is easy to use. However, the **mailx** program, which is an implementation of the Berkeley **mail** program for System V, has additional features that are useful in sending messages across the network. The **.mailrc** file can be configured to make it easier to send mail across the network. We'll look at how to specify aliases for remote users and how use a variable to supply your own network address. See the **man** page on the **mailx** command (or on **mail** itself on Berkeley UNIX systems) for more information on other features.

Aliases

If you are frequently sending mail to a user on a remote system, you may benefit from giving him or her an alias. You specify the alias which you will use to refer to the remote user and the complete address of that user. Here is a list of examples:

```
alias sue newyork!iowa!sioux!sue
alias anne newyork!japan!anne
alias guys "waltham!johnW newyork!ken"
```

Obviously, you don't want the alias to conflict with users on your own system who might be recipients of mail from you. The list of aliases is placed in the **.mailrc** file in your home directory.

Now, when you send mail to *anne*, you need only type her alias. It will be expanded and the message forwarded to the remote system.

Sending Your Network Address

If you are sending remote mail messages to systems beyond the local network, you probably want to give the recipient an address to reply to your message.

You can define the variable **Sign** in **.mailrc** to have it include your network address. This gives you a quick way to include it in mail messages.

```
set Sign="Fred Caslon ( newyork!newton!fred )"
```

Now, when you are typing a mail message, enter ˜A at the beginning of a line and press RETURN to have this variable inserted in your message. There's also a variable named **sign** which simply allows you to define an alternative, which can be read in with ˜a.

Transferring Binary Files

The **uuencode** and **uudecode** commands allow encoding and decoding of binary files for transmission through the **mail** program. These commands are available only on Berkeley systems or its derivatives, and some versions of System V offering Berkeley enhancements. Check the *UNIX Programmer's Guide* at your site to see if these commands are available on your system.

uuencode

uuencode is a special UUCP command for sending binary files to a remote system via **mail**. The syntax is:

> **uuencode** [*source*] *dest* | **mail** *sys!user*

uuencode takes input from the standard input or from a named *source* file and produces an encoded version of the file on the standard output, which can then be mailed to the remote system. The encoding converts the binary file to ASCII characters, and includes a header listing the mode of the file and the *dest*ination file on the remote system. For example,

```
% uuencode bnry /usr/mary/bnry | mail calif\!mary
%
```

mails an encoded version of the file *bnry* in your present working directory to *mary* on system *calif*. The encoded file has an ordinary text form and can be edited by **uudecode** or manually by any text editor to change the mode or the remote name.

uudecode

When *mary* reads her mail, she should save the encoded message in a file, and then decode it with **uudecode**. **uudecode** strips off any leading or trailing lines and characters used by **uuencode**. The syntax is:

> **uudecode** *file*

uudecode recreates the original file with the specified mode and name.

If **uudecode** is not available on your system, you can decode the binary file manually. The encoded file consists of a header line, followed by a number of body lines, and a trailer line. The header line contains three items separated by a blank: the word "begin", a mode (in octal), and the remote file name. The trailer line consists of the word "end."

The body contains a number of lines, each 62 characters long at most. Each line consists of a character count, followed by encoded characters and a newline. Refer to the **uuencode** command in the *UNIX Programmer's Manual* for the format of the encoded file.

Forwarding Files

Mail messages are not the only items that can be forwarded over the UUCP network. In theory, you can also transfer files to systems that are not directly linked to yours using an extended system pathname in **uucp**. In practice, forwarding by **uucp** seldom succeeds.

In Version 2, a file named FWDFILE must be set up to explicitly grant forwarding privileges. The systems that make up the indirect link must be willing to forward your file. In addition, such a request forwarded must originate in */usr/spool/uucppublic* or any public directory designated by your system administrator, and be sent to the public directory on the final destination system. Even then, it might fail if all the systems in the link did not run the same release of UUCP.

Berkeley 4.3 BSD has a program called **uusend** designed to handle extended remote pathnames. It presumes forwarding between Berkeley UNIX systems and access to the **uusend** command on each system.

BNU has improved its handling of forwarding requests. It uses **uux** to generate a **uucp** command on the forwarding system. The remote systems in the forwarding path must allow the **uucp** to be executed. Because of the different approach taken by each UUCP implementation, forwarding can occur only between systems running the same version of UUCP. (This is in addition to any intentional restrictions on forwarding put in place by the administrators of each system.)

If you want to send a copy of the file called *proposal* to a user named *deng* on *china*, you would enter:

```
% uucp ~/proposal newyork\!japan\!china\!~/deng
%
```

This sends a request to copy the file called *proposal* in */usr/spool/uucppublic* to system *newyork* that is linked to the local system *newton*. System *newyork* then forwards it (hopefully) to system *japan* (linked to *newyork* but not to *newton*), which then forwards it to */usr/spool/uucppublic/deng* on the destination system *china*. You can also use the **-m** and **-n** options of **uucp** to notify you and *deng* of a successful copy.

> NOTE: There are significant restrictions on forwarding of both files and mail over indirect UUCP links. Whenever you use Usenet, you are using the resources of other people who don't even know you.

For example, if you were to attempt to forward a large file (say 300K bytes) across the net, you could tie up the phone lines on *each* forwarding system for an hour and a half (1200 baud = 120 bytes/sec, including start and stop bits). This works out to about 7K bytes per minute, so a 300K file would require 45 minutes to receive, and 45 minutes to forward, at each site in the path to the final destination. Even apart from the inconvenience of having a system resource like a modem tied up for that amount of time, some links are made over long distance phone lines, so you are asking other people to foot *your* bill.

As it turns out, the forwarding software on many systems will reject mail messages larger than 100K, and 64K bytes is generally considered the outer limit on file size for mail forwarding. If you want to transmit large amounts of data, you should try to set up a direct phone link to the site in question. Then you are the only site to foot the bill.

Even for acceptably large transmissions, consider posting large or numerous mail messages late at night to take advantage of lower long distance rates and off-hours.

A considerable body of "net etiquette" has grown up regarding proper and improper use of the net. See the additional discussion of this topic in Chapters 7 and 8, *Using Netnews* and *Reading News*, before sending mail or forwarding files.

Transferring Multiple Files or Directory Hierarchies

Occasionally, you will find yourself faced with the need to transfer a large number of files, or even worse, an entire directory hierarchy. Particularly if you are restricted to the public directory, this can be quite awkward.

There are a couple of simple tricks that you can use to combine multiple files into a single file for transmission purposes.

1. First create a list of the files to be included. You can do this either manually or with a program like **ls** or **find**.

2. Use either of the backup programs **cpio** or **tar** to create an archive on standard output rather than on a backup device.

3. Redirect standard output to a file, then use UUCP to send the archive.

4. Use the same backup program on the target system to restore the archive.

For example, using **find** and **cpio**:

```
newton% find . -print | cpio -oc > archive.cpio
```

or using a manually-generated list of filenames:

```
newton% cpio -oc < filelist > archive.cpio
```

Then, after transferring *archive.cpio*, the remote system, with **uucp**, restores the archive:

```
waltham% cpio -icd < archive.cpio
```

(The **-c** option of **cpio** writes header information in ASCII for portability; **-d** tells **cpio** to create directories if needed when doing the restore; **-i** and **-o** are used, respectively, to copy files in and out.)

A similar example using **tar** might be:

```
newton% tar cf archive.tar `cat filelist`
        .
        .
        .
waltham% cat archive.tar | tar xf -
```

If you are not familiar with the use of **find, cpio** or **tar,** you may want to consult the appropriate command pages in the *UNIX Programmer's Manual* before trying out these commands.

7

Using Netnews

Getting on the Net
Net Articles and Newsgroups
Getting Started

Usenet is a worldwide network of computers that run the netnews software. As described earlier, Usenet is a public forum for the exchange of ideas in the form of news articles that are broadcast to member sites. Net users can post articles, reply by mail or send followup articles to previous ones, or simply read the news using the netnews programs.

The news messages that one gets on the net are as diverse as the persons who send them. To bring some structure into this collection of users and their ideas, news articles are classified into newsgroups.

When your system administrator sets up netnews, he or she may have decided to limit the number of newsgroups that your site will receive and broadcast. You can also define a personal list of newsgroups that you want to read so that you don't need to wade through newsgroups that you aren't interested in.

☐ Find out what newsgroups are available at your site.

☐ Draw up a list of newsgroups to which you would like to subscribe.

Getting on the Net

The companion handbook, *Managing UUCP and Usenet*, describes installing the netnews software to set up a link into the Usenet network. Obviously, this must be done if your site is to receive news.

Probably the easiest and best way to get on the net is to sign up with UUNET, a non-profit, commercial UUCP and Usenet hookup, originally funded by Usenix, the UNIX techical user's group. UUNET allows you to access the net via the Tymnet or CompuServe public data networks, which have local access phone numbers in most major cities. The off-peak (evening and weekend) connect charges for Tymnet are quite reasonable—$5/hour. CompuServe is $5/hour any time.

Alternatively, you can arrange to dial up directly, which may be more efficient if you are using high-speed Telebit Trailblazer modems. (The Trailblazer is optimized for use with UUCP, and is in general use at UUNET.)

Usenix estimates that the monthly cost of a full news feed is about $250, in addition to the UUNET membership fee of $35/month. The advantage is that you will be hooked in one hop from a backbone site. UUNET also offers an extensive collection of freely redistributable UNIX source archives.

You don't need to subscribe to UUNET to be able to use their archives via UUCP. By calling 1-900-468-7727 and using the login "uucp" with no password, anyone may uucp any of UUNET's on line source collection. (Start by copying *uunet!/usr/spool/ftp/ls-lR.Z*, which is a compressed index of every file in the archives.) As of this writing, the cost is 40 cents per minute. The charges will appear on your next telephone bill.

For more information, contact:

UUNET Communications Services
3110 Fairview Park Drive, Suite 570
P.O. Box 2324
Falls Church, VA 22042
+1 703 876-5050
info@uunet.uu.net
uunet!info

Net Articles and Newsgroups

The articles on the net are classified into *newsgroups*, according to subject matter. You can think of a newsgroup as a bulletin board or forum devoted to one topic. There are hundreds of newsgroups on the net that cater to every need or mood: newsgroups on technical topics such as artificial intelligence, programming language standards, or particular computer systems, as well as newsgroups for gardening, bugs (the computer kind) or wine. A listing of the current newsgroups as of fall 1989 is provided in Appendix D.

As of November 1986, newsgroups are divided into seven major categories,* as indicated by the first part of their names:

comp - Groups relating to some aspect of computer science (e.g., *comp.ai*).

sci - Groups relating to sciences other than computer science (e.g., *sci.physics* or *sci.math.symbolic*).

news - Groups relating to the netnews software (e.g.,*news.admin*) or of general interest to all net users (e.g., *news.announce*).

rec - Groups relating to recreational activities (e.g., *rec.arts.sf-lovers* or *rec.games.chess*).

---

*Before this date, there were only two categories: *net*, consisting of groups to which anyone could post, and *mod*, consisting of groups in which postings had first to be approved by a moderator. The recent division of newsgroups into seven categories was done for the express purpose of helping sites to exclude groups they don't want to carry.

soc -   Groups for social interaction or discussion of social topics (e.g.. *soc.singles* or *soc.culture.jewish*).

talk -   Groups prone to extended heated discussion (e.g., *talk.religion* or *talk.politics*).

misc -   Groups that don't fit into any of the other categories (e.g., *misc.jobs.offered* for job postings).

In addition, there may be one or more local newsgroups that are available only in your local area. There may also be groups found only at your site. One of these, called *general*, is almost certain to exist.

In addition to the standard seven hierarchies, and local or regional groups, there are several alternative hierarchies. These are created by groups of people who agree to carry and distribute these groups, independently of the standard hierarchies. Some of the major hierarchies are:

alt -   Short for "alternative." The original alternative hierarchy. A major feature is that anyone may create any group they please. Major groups include *alt.gourmand, alt.aquaria*, and *alt.sources*.

gnu -   A set of groups devoted to the Free Software Foundations GNU project.

pubnet - Groups devoted to the interests of public access UNIX sites.

bionet - Groups devoted to the exchange of biological information.

A brief description of each of the currently available net-wide newsgroups is usually kept in */usr/lib/news/newsgroups*. (Your system administrator might have installed the netnews software in another directory than /usr/lib/news, so inquire if you don't find this file.)

There are currently over 500 active newsgroups. However, your system administrator may not have subscribed to every newsgroup, since keeping all newsgroups can considerably increase telephone traffic and disk space usage. (In particular, *soc* and *talk* groups are not carried by many sites.) However, all groups will be listed in the *newsgroups* file, since it is a mirror image of another file, the *active* file, that the system uses to keep track of which messages have already been received at this site, and which should be rejected.

After looking over the *newsgroups* file, you may want to check with your system administrator to find out what groups are actually available. It is relatively easy to pick up a newsgroup that is requested by users, so don't be afraid to ask for a group your system doesn't ordinarily carry.

As mentioned above, there are also some local newsgroups whose names begin with a distribution prefix that restricts the distribution of the newsgroup to certain geographical areas or organizations. For example, the prefix "ne." in the newsgroup *ne.wanted* indicates that it will only be distributed to sites in New England. Some prefixes that are commonly used are given below. State-wide distribution prefixes usually take the two-letter abbreviation for that state (for example, "ca." for California only).

Table 7-1: Some Local Newsgroup Name Prefixes

Prefix	Distribution
att.	AT&T
can.	Canada
na.	North America
usa.	United States
ne.	New England
	Similar prefixes exist for other regions

A newsgroup name begins with one of the seven category names given above, or one of the local distribution names, followed by a dot (.) and the name of the main group. Newsgroups can also have subgroups. For example, *news.announce.newusers* is a subgroup of *news.announce*. While *news.announce* contains general articles that might be interesting for everyone on the net, *news.announce.newusers* has a specific audience in mind.

Getting Started

The volume of news is enormous. It is almost a certainty that you will not want to subscribe to every newsgroup—or even a significant fraction of the total.

You can specify which newsgroups you want to read by specifying command line options to the program you use for reading news. You can also save these options as a kind of personal subscription list in the file *.newsrc* in your home directory. This file is used by the news software to keep track of what articles you have read, as well as which newsgroups you want to read.

This file is created automatically the first time you try to read news, although the procedure differs depending on which of the news interface programs you use. (There are three programs for reading news in common use: **readnews** and **vnews** are part of the netnews distribution; **rn** is an optional program available at many sites.)

Creating *.newsrc* With **readnews**

Details of how to use the three programs for reading news are given in the next chapter. For the moment, let's assume you plan to use **readnews**, which is in many ways the most basic of the three programs.

The first time you invoke **readnews**, you should automatically be shown the newsgroup **general**. If your netnews administrator has followed the installation instructions, you should see something like this:

```
% readnews

- - - - - - - - - - - - - - - - -
Newsgroup general
- - - - - - - - - - - - - - - - -

Article 1 of 4, Nov 16  01:33.
Subject: Rules for posting to Usenet
Path: ..!ora!tim (Tim O'Reilly @ O'Reilly & Associates, Inc.)
(14 lines)  More? [ynq] y

This group contains several articles that you should
read in full before using the net.
```

Article 2 contains a paper by Mark Horton entitled "How to Read the Network News." You'll need this to get started.

Article 3 contains a piece by Matt Bishop entitled "How to Use Usenet Effectively." This article answers frequently asked questions about the net, and even more importantly, provides some guidelines about posting to the net. Do not use postnews before reading this article!

Article 4 contains a useful piece on copyright law by Jordan Breslow.

You can go on and read the articles in *general* by typing **y** at the "[ynq]" prompt each time it is shown to you. After you have finished reading (or right away if you want to get on with setting up the *.newsrc* file), type **q** to quit **readnews**. (Reading news is discussed in the next chapter.)

If you get the message "no news", then *general* was empty. Your *.newsrc* file will not be set up either. Try again, this time using the **-n** option to specify the newsgroups you want to read. The easiest thing to do is to type:

```
% readnews -n all
```

Then type **q** to quit without reading news. *.newsrc* should now contain a complete newsgroup list. Let's see what it might look like:

```
% cd
% more .newsrc
comp.ai:
comp.ai.digest:
comp.arch:
comp.bugs.2bsd:
comp.bugs.4bsd:
       .
       .
       .
```

Your *.newsrc* file contains the entire list of active newsgroups. Each newsgroup name is followed by a colon. If you have actually read one or more articles, the colon will be followed by the numbers of the articles in the newsgroup that you have actually read. (This is how the software keeps from showing you the same article over again.)

Modifying *.newsrc*

Many of the newsgroups listed in *.newsrc* may not be of interest to you. In addition to keeping track of which articles you have already read, *.newsrc* can also be used as your personal subscription list.

As mentioned above, the programs for reading news take a number of options for specifying which articles you want to read. You can specify newsgroups, titles, or the date of articles. However, in most cases, you want to look at a number of different newsgroups, and don't want to have to type a lot of command line options.

You can add an "options" line as the first line of *.newsrc*, and the options on that line will be executed just as if they had been typed on the command line when you invoke a program to read news.

To select which newsgroups you want to read, start the first line of the file with the word "options" and specify the **-n** *neimportant.roups* option, just as you would when invoking the **readanews** or **vnews** command.

> **NOTE:** As a new user, it is highly recommended that you subscribe to *news.announce.newusers* and *news.announce. important.news.announce.newusers* contains articles relating to proper conduct on the net. These articles are akin to a beginner's primer on Usenet. *news.announce.important* is used for occasional very important announcements.

When using **options**, you can specify the newsgroups you want, or don't want—whichever is easier. An exclamation point preceding the newsgroup name means you don't want to see it. To specify all sub-groups within a group, you can specify "all" following the name of the newsgroup. (For example, *comp.all* means all *comp* groups. *all* by itself means all groups.)

If the list goes over more than one line, begin subsequent lines with spaces or tabs, and they will be treated as continuation lines.

For example, you might include an options line like this:

```
options -n news.all comp.sources.unix comp.text
```

This line will subscribe to all groups in the *news* category plus the two specific groups *comp.sources.unix* (public domain UNIX software) and *comp.text* (text processing).

Or you could specify an options line like this:

```
options -n all !talk.all !soc.all !rec.all \
    !sci.astro !comp.bugs.2bsd !comp.bugs.4bsd
                      .
                      .
                      .
```

This line will subscribe to all groups except the groups listed with exclamation points. Note that you cannot simply specify a list of groups that you don't want without specifying some that you do want. The exclamation point is generally used in this case to specify subgroups that you don't want within a general group that you do want to see.

If you are planning to specify a long list of groups that you do or don't want, there is another way of doing this that may be easier in the long run:

1. Specify the options line **options -n all** at the start of *.newsrc*.
2. Start reading news. Just read enough of each newsgroup to see if it interests you (otherwise you'll be there forever). If you want to subscribe, type **N** to jump to the next newsgroup. If you never want to see the newsgroup again, there is a command to unsubscribe. Unfortunately, it differs for each of the three news-reading programs. In **readnews**, type **U**, in **vnews**, type **ug**, and in **rn**, type **u**.
3. Alternatively, you can go down the list of newsgroup names in *.newsrc*, and insert an exclamation point instead of a colon immediately following each newsgroup name that you don't want to see. For example:

```
misc.wanted!
```

means that you have unsubscribed to *misc.wanted*. Changing the "!" character back to a ":" renews your subscription to this group.

Order of Newsgroups

On many systems, newsgroups are presented in the order in which they appear in *.newsrc*. You may want to sort *.newsrc* so that the newsgroups you are most interested in are at the front of the file.

The newsgroups are initially listed in the order in which they appear in your system's *active* file. Your system administrator may have already ordered this file to put important groups first; however, by default, they are listed in alphabetical order.

Creating *.newsrc* With **rn**

If you plan to use **rn** to read news (see the next chapter for details), you can let **rn** prompt you for a list of newsgroups you want to subscribe to. It automatically runs the **newsetup** program and creates the *.newsrc* file if it doesn't exist the first time you invoke **rn**. If *.newsrc* already exists, it makes a backup copy called *.oldnewsrc*.

```
% rn
Trying to set up a .newsrc file--running newsetup...

Creating .newsrc in /usr/john to be used by news programs.
Done.

If you have never used the news system before, you may
find the articles in news.announce.newusers to be
helpful.  There is also a manual entry for rn.

To get rid of newsgroups you aren't interested in, use
the 'u' command.  Type h for help at any time while
running rn.

%
```

The **u** command in **rn** will automatically append an exclamation point after the name of each newsgroup you select for "unsubscription". *rn* also includes a command to reorder the *.newsrc* for you.

8

Reading News
Programs for Reading News
Reading News With **rn**
Finding Out Where You Are

Once you have set up your personal subscription list, you can start reading some of the news in your newsgroups. Let's assume that your *.newsrc* file has been set up as described in the previous chapter.

There are three commands used to read news: **vnews, readnews** and **rn**. (**rn** may not be available at your site. Currently, the standard distribution has **readnews** and **vnews**, but not **rn**.)

In this chapter, you will learn how to:

☐ Read news using **vnews, readnews** and **rn**.

☐ Display a listing of articles in a newsgroup.

☐ Choose a newsgroup or article to read.

☐ Save an article in a file.

Note that this chapter is designed to introduce you to the topic of reading netnews, and does not present all of the options available with each of these programs. After you have used the netnews software for a while, you should get a copy of the *man* pages for **readnews** and **rn**, which present additional details. These pages may be available on-line with the **man** command, or you can ask your system administrator for a copy.

Programs for Reading News

The **vnews**, **readnews** and **rn** programs differ in the number of options they allow. They also differ in style and speed. (**readnews** is not screen oriented. **vnews** is faster than **rn** for some things, slower for others.) This affects their ease of use and flexibility in moving through newsgroups and articles. But there are some basic similarities among them, and they are summarized here:

- When you invoke any of these programs, the first unread article of the first newsgroup in your *.newsrc* file will be displayed. So, it is good practice to reorder your newsgroups so that the more important ones are listed first.

- A news article is said to be *read* if you go through the entire article. However, there are commands that allow you to mark an article as read without actually going through it, or to mark it as *unread* when you have actually finished reading it. Once an article is read, you normally cannot go back and reread it the next time you invoke any of these programs.

- These programs use a paging program to break the article into pages. You can use some of the pager's commands to control your movement through the file.

A news article always consists of two parts: the header and the body of the news. The header lists some or all of the following information:

- Article number in the newsgroup. Each article received at your site is automatically assigned a number.

- Network address of the sender.

- Newsgroup(s) to which it belongs.
- Subject.
- Usenet message ID.
- Date sent by the author.
- Date received at your site.
- Name of the organization from which it was sent.
- Number of lines in the body of the text.

A Word About Options

The three news-handling programs take quite a few different command line options. As suggested above, you will eventually want to read the *man* pages for each program, since there may be options you want to experiment with.

However, there is one useful set of options that **readnews** and **vnews** have in common. These options give you more control over what you want to read than is given by *.newsrc*. They include:

-n *newsgroups*	Only show articles in *newsgroups*. If you specify more than one newsgroup, groups in the list should be separated by spaces, not commas.
-t *titles*	Only show articles with *titles*. You don't need to remember the exact title. *titles* is any string that is contained in the title, so you can search for a keyword or two, if you like.
-a [*date*]	Only show articles more recent than *date*. *date* should be in *mm/dd/yy* format.
-x	Ignore the list of already-read articles in *.newsrc*. That is, show all news, even if it has previously been read. This option is generally used together with one of the other options.
-K	Mark all articles as read, whether they've been seen or not. This option is sometimes useful when you're starting out, since it allows you to ignore the accumulation of old news and read what comes in on a day-to-day basis.

You can also use these options (except **-K**) with **checknews,** a program that simply reports whether or not there is news. For example:

```
% checknews -n comp.lang.pascal
There is news.
```

If there is no news, **checknews** will return without printing any message.

vnews

Once *.newsrc* has been set up, **vnews** can be invoked without any arguments:

```
% vnews

Newsgroup news.announce

Article <502@cbosgd.UUCP> Nov 16 06:36
Subject: results of call-for-papers poll
Path: ..!cbosgd!mark
(49 lines)


more?          news.announce 69/112    Nov 16 1:33
```

In the first 22 lines of the first page, **vnews** displays the name of the newsgroup, then the header of the first unread article. It then prompts you ("**more?**") for what to do next. Press RETURN to see the next page, or the next unread article when you have read the current one. Press "**n**" if you want to go to the next article without reading the current article. The last line also tells you that the current article is number 69 out of 112 articles in this newsgroup. It also prints today's date and time. When you reach the end of the article, **vnews** will prompt you with "**next?**".

The other commonly-used commands of **vnews** are given below. Note that you do not have to press RETURN after entering a command. Enter "**?**" at any time to get a complete menu of **vnews** commands online.

Table 8-1: Some **vnews** Command Options

Command	Description
e	Mark current news as unread.
+*x*	Go forward *x* article.
-	Go to previous article.
A#	Select article by number #
p	Go back to parent article (the last article this is a followup to). Toggle between parent and current article with -.
x^B	Go backward *x* pages.
x^N	Go forward *x* lines.
x^P	Go backward *x* lines.
s *file*	Save article in *file*.
r or R	Post a reply to the article you just read. (See Chapter 8 first.)
<esc>R	Reply by mail to an article.
N *news*	Go to named *news*group.
ug	Unsubscribe to this newsgroup.

To get out of **vnews**, press "q". **vnews** automatically goes to the next newsgroup when you've read all previously unread articles in the current newsgroup.

readnews

readnews is similar to **vnews**. After the header is displayed, you get the prompt "[ynq]". The main difference is that **readnews** is line oriented, while **vnews** is screen oriented.

```
% readnews

- - - - - - - - - - - - - -
Newsgroup news.announce
- - - - - - - - - - - - - -
```

```
Article 69 of 112, Nov 16   01:33.
Subject: results of call-for-papers poll
Path: ..!cbosgd!mark (Mark Horton @ Bell Labs, Columbus)
(49 lines)   More? [ynq] y
[First, I'd like to correct the previous article. Due to
                           .
                           .
--MORE--(87%)
```

After displaying the header, **readnews** gives a **more** prompt and three command options that have the same meaning as in **vnews**. In the above example, we entered "y" (for "yes") so **vnews** displayed the first page of the article. At the bottom of the first page, you get another **more** prompt for your next action. Press RETURN to see the rest of the article.

Some of the commands of **readnews** are listed below. The "?" key gives a menu of the **readnews** commands online.

Table 8-2: Some **readnews** Commands

Command	Description
n	No. Go to next article.
#	Go to article number # in the current newsgroup.
q	Quit this newsgroup.
U	Unsubscribe from this newsgroup.
N *[news]*	Go to named *news*group. Default is next newsgroup.
s *[file]*	Append article to *file*. Default is "Articles".
r	Reply by **mail** to the author of the article. (See Chapter 8 first.)
e	Mark this article as unread.
-	Go back to last article.
b	Back up one article in current newsgroup.
K	Mark remaining articles in this group as read.
v	Print current news version number.

rn

rn is a more complex program that claims to reduce the "dead" time you spend in deciding whether to read an article or not. It is not a part of the standard netnews distribution, but may be available on some systems. It gives you the flexibility to move in and out of articles and newsgroups and perform other tasks such as pattern-matching using regular expressions. The syntax is:

rn [*option*] [*newsgroups*]

You can enter **rn** alone or with a named newsgroup.

rn lets you enter commands at three levels: the *newsgroup selection level*, the *article selection level* (within the newsgroup), and the *pager* level (within the article). All three levels have their own prompts, commands and a menu of these commands. We will describe only some of these commands since you can press "**h**" at any time in order to get a menu of the commands at each level.

When you invoke **rn**, it first looks for your *.newsrc* file, performs some consistency checks on it, and then checks whether new newsgroups have been created that are not in your file. It then prompts you if you want to add these newsgroups to your *.newsrc* file.

```
% rn
                    ***RN NEWS***
                         .
                         .
                         .
Checking out your .newsrc--hang on a second...

Checking active list for new newsgroups...

Newsgroup talk.rumors not in .newsrc -- add?  [yn] n

Put newsgroup where?  h
                         .
                         .
                         .
Newsgroup comp.mac.sources not in .newsrc -- add? [yn]
```

Typing "n" (without a RETURN) implies that you want to ignore this newsgroup. **rn** then prompts you for the next unlisted new newsgroup. Typing "y" or a SPACE BAR indicates that the newsgroup is to be added to *.newsrc*. (Whenever you are given the option in brackets, the default is given first. Typing SPACE BAR means to use the default.)

The new newsgroup is simply appended to the end of the existing *.newsrc* file. Type "h", as we have done above, to get a menu of commands if you want to change the order of the newsgroups. **rn** will go on prompting you until it runs out of new newsgroups.

Reading News With rn

If there are no newsgroups, **rn** goes directly to the newsgroup selection level. It displays the number of unread articles in your newsgroups, and then asks you if you want to start reading the articles in the first newsgroup.

```
% rn
Unread news in news.announce          5 articles
Unread news in news.misc              9 articles
        .
        .
        .

    **** 5 unread articles in news.announce--read now? [ynq]
```

The last line is the prompt at the newsgroup selection level. The three command options have the following meaning.

Table 8-3: Prompts at the Newsgroup Level

Prompt	Description
y	Read this newsgroup now. Also SPACE BAR .
n	Go to the next newsgroup.
q	Quit the **rn** program.

Note that you do not press RETURN after entering the options at this prompt.

Listing the Articles

It is sometimes useful to list the subject headings in the newsgroup and then decide if you actually want to go through this newsgroup or not. You can get a listing by pressing the equal sign (=) at the newsgroup prompt, as in the example below:

```
*****   5 unread articles in news.announce--read now?
        [ynq] =

 85   results of call-for-papers poll
110   Newsgroup conversion is proceeding
111   "soc" and "talk" groups coming out soon
112   Creating new groups

What next? [npq]
```

You can then enter the article number you want at the "**What next?**" prompt or press "**q**" to quit this newsgroup. "**p**" displays the previous article. Note that, in our listing, articles 86 to 109 have been skipped. These articles have been read or have been deleted by your system administrator.

A partial listing of immediately useful commands is given in the following table.

Table 8-4: Some Commands at the Newsgroup Level

Command	Description
u	Unsubscribe from this newsgroup.
n	Go to next newsgroup with unread news.
N	Go to next newsgroup.
p	Go to previous newsgroup with unread news.
P	Go to previous newsgroup.
$	Go to the end of the newsgroups list.
L	List the current state of *.newsrc*.

Reading a Named Newsgroup

Instead of having **rn** go through each newsgroup down your *.newsrc* list, you can go directly to the newsgroup of your choice. This is done in two ways:

1. Give the newsgroup name when you invoke **rn**. **rn** will first list the number of unread news in that newsgroup and all its subdirectories. You will also get the newsgroup level prompt.

2. Enter "**g** *newsgroup*" at the newsgroup level prompt.

Reading Articles

When you have selected the newsgroup you want to read, **rn** goes into the article selection level. By default, it prints out unread articles in the order in which they arrived at your site. You are **not** asked whether you want to read the article before it is displayed; **rn** simply displays the first page and asks if you want to continue.

```
% rn comp.sources.wanted
Unread news in comp.sources.wanted 13 articles

*****  13 unread articles in comp.sources.wanted--read
              now? [ynq] y

Article 172 (12 more) in comp.sources.wanted:
From: tim@ora.UUCP (Tim O'Reilly)
Newsgroups: comp.sources.wanted
Subject: Need example nroff terminal table
Message-ID: <921@ora.UUCP>
Date: 11 Nov 86 23:29:40 GMT
Organization: O'Reilly & Associates, Inc., Newton, MA
Lines: 15
Keywords: nroff term table
              .
              .
              .
--MORE--(61%)
```

The first line says that this is article 172 and that there are 12 more unread articles in this newsgroup. The last line is the prompt at the pager level. Press SPACE BAR to view the next page. At the end of the article, the following prompt appears:

```
End of article 172 (of 184) -- what next? [npq]
```

This is the article level prompt. Some of the commands you can enter at this point are given below.

Table 8-5: Some Commands at the Article Level

Command	Description
n	Go to the next unread article.
p	Go to the previous unread article.
q	Quit this newsgroup.
N	Go to next article.
P	Go to previous article.
-	Go to previously displayed article.
$	Go to last article.

You can also enter the above commands at the pager level prompt "—MORE—". In addition, you can move through the article using the pager commands given below.

Table 8-6: Some Commands at the Pager Level

Command	Description
d	Display one-half page more.
RETURN	Display one more line.
j	Mark this article as read and go to end of article.
b	Back up one page.
^L	Refresh screen.
q	Go to end of current article.

Choosing an Article

You can save a lot of time spent in reading the headers of all articles in a newsgroup by listing the subject headers. Press the equals sign ("=") at the article level prompt, just as you did earlier at the newsgroup level prompt, to get a subject listing. Then enter the number of the article you want to read.

```
                              .
                              .
                              .
    --MORE--(61%) End of article 172 (of 184)--what next?
                         [npq] 175
```

Entering an article number forces **rn** to go to the end of the current article. The current article is then left in an unread state.

Saving an Article

The s command at the article level allows you to save the news article in a named destination *file*. The form:

    s *file*

entered at the prompt saves the article in your news directory. If the file already exists, **rn** appends the article to it. Let's say that after reading Article 172, we decide to save the contents in a file called *term_request*.

```
                          .
                          .
                          .
    End of article 172 (of 184)--what next? [npq]
            s ./term_request

    File /usr/john/News/term_request doesn't exist--
        Use mailbox format? [ynq]
```

Pressing "**y**" saves the news in mailbox format; "**n**" saves it in normal (non-mailbox) format. To get out of this newsgroup, press "**q**".

The **w** command works the same way as the **s** command but saves the article without its header.

Finding Out Where You Are

When your site subscribed to Usenet, your system administrator should have notified *news.newsites* informing other systems on the network about your system and who you're linked to. A complete database of sites on the network is posted monthly to the newsgroup **comp.mail.maps**. Read this newsgroup to find out what systems are on the net. This will also come in handy when you learn how to post articles and want to send mail to a user on the net.

Note that a UUCP site may not necessarily be a Usenet site. File and mail transfers may occur over UUCP, but not necessarily news. Also, a Usenet site may not necessarily be a UUCP site. UUCP is the most common, but far from the only, method of transferring files.

Most likely, if your system has subscribed to this newsgroup, your system administrator has also picked up a version of a mail program that knows how to use this database to forward mail directly to another site without requiring you to specify an intervening path. Ask your system administrator for details.

9

Posting News

The Do´s and Don´ts of Net–Working
Posting New Articles
Replying to Articles
Sending Followups
A Last Word on Etiquette

The best way to learn how to post news is to watch what others are doing, then try it out for yourself. You probably have gone through several newsgroups and articles by now and have an idea of what is considered acceptable behavior on the net. Reading news may be the most popular activity for a majority of users on the net. But there may come a time when you feel the need to speak up—to clarify a point, to solicit opinions, to publicize a piece of technical information, or even to find a buyer for your '76 Mustang.

This chapter describes how to:

□ Post articles to the net using **postnews** and **Pnews**.

□ Reply to articles and send followups using the commands of **vnews**, **readnews** and **rn**.

But before you even attempt to write news for the net, make sure that you have read the articles in *news.announce.newusers*, in particular, the article, *How to Use the Usenet Effectively*.

The Do's and Don'ts of Net-Working

The members of the net are faceless names to us, and it is easy to get carried away in what we write or how we write. How often have you seen followups or replies that sound unprofessional? A number of major sites have actually dropped some of the newsgroups because the amount of drivel in some of them do not justify the cost of broadcasting the news to other sites "free of charge." The successful and productive use of the net rests on the assumption that its users have read and abide by the net etiquette.

Net etiquette is a set of guidelines that has evolved from the cumulative experience of thousands of net users. These guidelines make a lot of sense if you think through the logistics of the net. First, in order to reach each site on the net, an article is received and retransmitted hundreds of times. The cost of transmission is borne by the members of the net each time they forward a message. At major sites, both transmission costs and disk space usage can be considerable.

Second, considering the volume of traffic on the net, reading news can become quite a chore if you have to wade through numerous irrelevant messages in order to get to what you want.

There are some basic ground rules for preparing an article for the net. The following sections summarize these rules.

Limit Your Distribution

Think where your article is going and try local or regional groups first. If a car in Kalamazoo is for sale, it is unlikely that a reader in Korea would be interested. On the other hand, if you would like to participate in a discussion on UNIX standardization, you deserve to be heard by a greater number of people. The news posting program will ask you how widely your article should be distributed (more on this below); keep in mind that if you don't limit the distribution, your article will be broadcast worldwide.

Use the Correct Newsgroup

There are newsgroups for every topic under the sun; use them for the intention in which they were created. As much as possible, limit the number of newsgroups to which you post your article. Nobody wants to see the same news in more than one or two newsgroups, particularly when it is obvious that the sender is unsure about where it really belongs. Inappropriate announcements may cause your site to be removed from the net.

Some of the newsgroups are moderated, and some have their own rules about the content of discussion that is allowed. Modern netnews software automatically converts postings to moderated groups into mail to the moderator.

Define Your Subject

Most users base their decision to read the current article or not on the subject header. Thus, if you want to attract the attention of the right people, make your subject header specific. "76 Mustang For Sale" is okay; "76 Mustang For Sale in Kalamazoo, MI" is even better.

Product and service announcements are frowned upon on the net. If you have to, post such messages only once and do not use marketing hype. Also, mark your message as a product announcement. *comp.newprod* is the group where commercial announcements are normally posted.

Be Brief

This does not mean that you cut down on the articles "the", "an", and so on. This makes your message unreadable. Just make your news direct and to the point.

Make It Readable

It is good practice to write down your message first, or use a text editor so that you can check it for grammar, style and spelling. Avoid the use of sarcasm since it is easily misunderstood. Also, if you disagree with the author, *send mail* instead of replying to the net. Do not forget to give credit where credit is due.

Posting New Articles

There are two commands used for sending new articles to the net: **postnews** and **Pnews**. Both programs prompt you for some information and then automatically create a temporary news file using the default text editor (usually **vi**) defined by your system administrator.

postnews

A session on **postnews** is shown below and shows the prompts that you would get when you invoke this program.

```
% postnews
Is this message in response to some other message? n
Subject: Looking for local news feed in Newton, Mass.
Keywords:
Newsgroups (enter one at a time, end with a blank line):

The most relevant newsgroup should be the first, you
should add others only if your article really MUST be
read by people who choose not to read the appropriate
group for your article.  But DO use multiple
newsgroups rather than posting many times.

For a list of newsgroups, type ?
> ne.general
>
```

The first prompt is answerable only by "y" (yes), or "n" (*no*). If you respond with "n", **postnews** will then prompt you for the subject header. Press ⌐RETURN⌐ when you're done. **postnews** then asks you for the appropriate newsgroup where it will be posted, and how widely distributed you want your news. At this point, **postnews** invokes the text editor that is specified by your system administrator*, and creates a temporary news file.

```
Subject: Looking for local news feed in Newton, Mass.
Newsgroups: ne.general
```

---

*If you want to use an editor other than the default editor selected by your system administrator, setting the variable EDITOR in your environment will cause **postnews** to select that editor.

The header is automatically created and shows whatever you typed in at the prompts. You then create the text file and enter your message using the appropriate editor command for entering text. When you're done, use the editor command for saving the file. You will then get the following message:

```
What now? [send, edit, list, quit, write]
```

send will post the message. edit will reinvoke your editor on the message. list will print your message out on the screen invoking the default pager if necessary. quit will abort without posting the message. write allows you to save the message to a file. It will prompt for the filename.

```
Posting article ...
Article posted successfully.
```

Entering "**y**" in response to the first prompt is the same as sending a followup to an article. **postnews** will then ask you for the newsgroup you read the article in and the article number. An easier way to send a follow-up is to use the **f** command of **readnews**, **vnews** or **rn**, as described in a later section.

Pnews

Pnews is similar to **postnews**. It is not a part of the standard netnews distribution, but may be available on some systems. (It comes with **rn**.) The prompts that you will get are shown below:

```
% Pnews
I see you've never used this version of Pnews before.
                        .
                        .
                        .
Newsgroup(s):

Your local distribution prefixes are:
            State:          ne
            Country:        usa
            Continent:      na
            Everywhere:     world
Distribution (world):

Title/Subject:

This program may post news to many machines.
Are you absolutely sure you want to do this? [ny]
```

The "Newsgroup(s)" prompt allows you to enter one or more news-groups. If you want to post to more than one, you should do them all at once instead of sending a separate article to each newsgroup, since this will allow the netnews software to transmit only a single copy of the article. The "Distribution" prompt asks how widely distributed you want your article. Pressing [RETURN] indicates the default, in this case, the "net". Next, you enter your subject header.

Pnews also gives you a chance to back out before it creates the tempo-rary news file. Pressing "n" allows you to exit gracefully. If you enter "y", **Pnews** creates the file as in **postnews** and posts the article.

Signing Your Name

Both **postnews** and **Pnews** will automatically conclude your posting with the contents of the *.signature* file contained in your home direc-tory. This is useful for including "return address" information.

A *.signature* file might look like this:

```
ora:/usr2/tim/.signature
```

This file can be no more than four lines long, or it will not be used.

Replying to Articles

If you want to reply to another article, you should *send mail to the author*, and not broadcast your reply to the entire net. This cuts down on the number of articles that Usenet sites have to send, and even more importantly it cuts down on junk for people to read.

The **r** command of **vnews**, **readnews** and **rn** allows you to send replies through the net mail. These three commands are used in a similar way. When you enter "**r**" at the "More?" prompt of **vnews** or **readnews**, or at the article level prompt of **rn**, a file is automatically created with a header like the one below:

```
To: bloom-beacon!ora!tim
Subject: Re: troff bugs
In-reply-to: your article <1800004@ora.UUCP>
```

The program fills in the appropriate path and subject header. This information is taken from the header of the article you were reading or have just read when you entered the command. Use the text editor that is invoked to compose your reply.

Enter the "write" command on your editor when you're done. What happens then depends on the program. In **readnews, r** sends mail to the originator of the article. In **vnews** and **rn, r** posts an article to the net. (Use **<esc>r** in **vnews** to send mail.) *Be sure you want to post an article before you use this command in* **vnews** *or* **rn**. The net is often flooded with dozens of nearly identical replies to an article, due to trigger-happy readers. In many cases, it is preferable to reply by mail.

If you decide not to post your reply, use the "quit" command on your editor. A message similar to "**File not changed – no message posted**" will appear.

The **R** command of **vnews** and **rn** allows you to reply to the article as above, but also includes the current article to which you are replying in the header file that is generated. The variables that appear in the header can also be modified in **rn**. You should edit the copy of the original article that is included. This will reduce the amount of duplicate information people will have to read.

Sending Followups

To submit a followup article, use the **f** command of **vnews** and **readnews**, and the **F** command of **rn**. These commands automatically create a header and reprint the original article, with lines prefixed by ">".

```
Subject: Re: KSH, anyone?
Newsgroups: ne.general
References: <1800004@ora.UUCP>

>
>
```

```
> Has anyone in the Boston/Cambridge area got KSH
> up and running? Would they be willing and/or able
>               .
>               .
>               .
```

NOTE: Be sure to edit the copy of the previous article so that you are not sending out unnecessary text. Include text only when necessary, and even then quote only a few lines. (Modern versions of the news software will reject articles containing more than 50% included text.)

You can create your new article after the reprint. Use the editor command to save the file (for example, :wq in vi) and post the followup. If you change your mind, use the "quit" command on your editor. A system message similar to the following will appear:

```
File not modified - no message posted.
continue?
```

Pressing "n" gets you back to the original article; "y" lets you return to the temporary file. Use the f option of rn if you don't want to reprint the old article in your followup.

A Last Word on Etiquette

The rules for sending news may seem a lot, but they are all really based on common sense. There has been some discussion that the net is going the way of the dinosaurs; it has become too big, and there are really no "brains" or central control to speak of. Every time you send a message, you are relying on the goodwill, disk space, and phone bill of others who are willing to forward it for you. The importance of net etiquette becomes more apparent when you realize that the continued existence of the net requires the cooperation of everyone.

A

Useful Shell Scripts

This appendix contains a number of shell scripts that we've used to make life with UUCP easier. The script is presented followed by a command page that describes it. Here's a summary of the commands:

pubcheck   List public directory

uuget   Get files from public directory

The **pubcheck** Shell Script

```
if [ "$#" != "0" ]; then
    find /usr/spool/uucppublic -type f -print | grep $*;
else
    find /usr/spool/uucppublic -type f -print
fi
```

pubcheck	**List Public Directory**

SUMMARY

Lists all files that have been received and are waiting in
/usr/spool/uucppublic.

DESCRIPTION

pubcheck *pattern*

pubcheck is a useful aid for listing the files in the public directory.
This command by default lists all the files currently in the public directory. If you supply an argument, it will try to match that *pattern* to the
pathnames.

EXAMPLE

```
% pubcheck
/usr/spool/uucppublic/receive/dale/eg1
/usr/spool/uucppublic/adrian/attlist
/usr/spool/uucppublic/laurel/macstuff
/usr/spool/uucppublic/mary/plans.john
/usr/spool/uucppublic/mary/report

% pubcheck mary
/usr/spool/uucppublic/mary/plans.john
/usr/spool/uucppublic/mary/report
```

The **uuget** Shell Script

```
FILES=""
if [ "$1" ]; then
    SOURCE=$1
    PUBDIR=/usr/spool/uucppublic/$SOURCE
else
    PUBDIR=/usr/spool/uucppublic/$LOGNAME
fi
if [ "$2" ]; then
    DESTINATION=$2
elif [ -d "$SOURCE" ]; then
    DESTINATION=$SOURCE
    PUBDIR=/usr/spool/uucppublic/$LOGNAME
else
    DESTINATION="."
fi
if [ -d "$PUBDIR" ]; then
    echo $PUBDIR":"
    ls -Fx $PUBDIR
    echo
    echo "To move All files, Select files or do Nothing,"
    echo "Enter [A/S/N]\c:"
    read input
    case $input in
        A*|a*) for q in `ls -F $PUBDIR | grep -v "/"`;
        do
        FILES="$FILES $PUBDIR/$q";
        done;;
        S*|s*) echo "Confirm files you want moved: [Y/N/Q]";
            for x in `ls -F $PUBDIR | grep -v "/"`;
        do
        echo "$x :\c";
        read answer;
        case $answer in
            Y*|y*) FILES="$FILES $PUBDIR/$x";;
            Q*|q*) exit;;
            N*|n*|*) continue;;
        esac
        done;;
            N*|n*|*)  exit;;
    esac
elif [ -f "$PUBDIR" ]; then
    FILES=$PUBDIR
else
```

```
    echo $PUBDIR "does not exist"; exit
fi
if [ "$FILES" ]; then
    mv $FILES $DESTINATION
else
    echo "uuget: No Source File"
fi
```

Get Files from Public Directory	uuget

SUMMARY

Move files from the public directory to current directory or other location on file system.

DESCRIPTION

uuget [*source*[*destination*]]

source is the name of a subdirectory or file in the public directory. *destination* is the pathname of a directory to which the files will be moved.

If *source* is not supplied, then the program looks for a subdirectory that matches your login user id (LOGNAME). If *source* is a subdirectory, the program lists that directory and asks you whether you want to move all or some of the files. (The program does not attempt to move subdirectories of this directory.)

```
To move All files, Select files or do Nothing,
Enter [A/S/N]
```

If you want to select files, you will be prompted to answer Yes or No for each file.

If *source* is a file in the public directory, it will be moved to the destination without prompting.

If the destination directory is not supplied, the source files are moved to the current working directory. Absolute or relative pathnames can be used.

As shown in the last example below, the destination can be supplied as a single argument to the **uuget** command. The only stipulation is that this argument cannot also be a subdirectory off the public directory. (The default *source* directory is used.) Absolute pathnames help to make sure this argument is interpreted as a destination. Relative pathnames will work. However, the program checks to see if it can be the pathname of a subdirectory or file off the public directory. Thus, if there is a subdirectory of the public directory named *vmark*, I could not refer to a subdirectory off my current directory named *vmark*. I could do it using an absolute pathname, as shown below:

```
% uuget /work/vmark
```

EXAMPLES

Without arguments, **uuget** lists the files in the appropriate subdirectory of the public directory and asks you to take an action. You can move all or some files to the current working directory or do nothing.

```
% uuget
/usr/spool/uucppublic/dale:
status          takeme          takeme.too

To move All files, Select files or do Nothing,
Enter [A/S/N]s
Confirm files you want moved: [Y/N/Q]
status :n
takeme :y
takeme.too :n
```

The result is that the file */usr/spool/uucppublic/dale/takeme* is copied into the current working directory.

The next example supplies an argument that is interpreted as a subdirectory of the public directory. The file(s) in that directory is listed and again you are prompted to act. Answering "A" or "a" moves all the files in that directory to the current directory.

```
% uuget laurel
/usr/spool/uucppublic/laurel:
macstuff

To move All files, Select files or do Nothing,
Enter [A/S/N]a
```

The file */usr/spool/uucppublic/laurel/macstuff* is moved into the current working directory.

The next example shows two arguments. The first is the source directory off the public directory and the second is the absolute or relative pathname of the destination directory.

```
% uuget adrian /work/dale
/usr/spool/uucppublic/adrian:
attlist

To move All files, Select files or do Nothing,
Enter [A/S/N]a
```

The result is that the file /usr/spool/uucppublic/adrian/attlist is copied into the directory /work/dale.

You can supply a single argument and have it interpreted as the destination directory instead of the source directory. This example shows how the first argument, if it can be interpreted as an existing directory, will be taken to be the destination for the copy. The first argument is not interpreted as a subdirectory of the public directory and the default, the user's LOGNAME, is used.

```
% uuget /work/dale
/usr/spool/uucppublic/dale:
status          takeme          takeme.too

To move All files, Select files or do Nothing,
Enter [A/S/N]a
```

This command moves three files from the public directory into the directory /work/dale.

B

The Spool Directory

When a UUCP job is entered, files are created in a spool directory for processing by UUCP background programs (or daemons). In the spool directory, there are log files, which are added to each time a transfer occurs, and a number of working files that are dynamically created in the course of communication between systems.

The pathname of the spool directory is */usr/spool/uucp*. One of the major improvements of BNU over Version 2 is the introduction of a more organized spool directory. We'll look at the spool directory for Version 2 and describe the various files that are found there.

Here's a listing of a spool directory:

```
% ls -x /usr/spool/uucp
AUDIT          C.naticknA5695    D.newtonXA5584    LCK..tty006
LCK..natick    LOGDEL            LOGFILE           LTMP.23066
Log-WEEK       STST.natick       SYSLOG            X.califX05tA
o.Log-WEEK     o.SYSLOG.
```

Work (*C*.) Files. When a user issues a **uucp** command, what actually happens is that a *work file* is created in the spool directory. The work file contains the instructions for **uucico** such as the name of the file to be copied, its owner and permissions, its destination, and so on.

All work file names begin with the characters *C.*. The name also contains the remote system name, the job id and other control information.

Data (*D*.) Files. A data file normally contains If the user specifies **uucp**'s -C option, the actual file is copied to the spool directory as well. The copy is kept in a *data file* which has the prefix *D.*, and is otherwise named just like the work file it is associated with. When a user sends mail, two data files are created — one containing the text of the mail message, the other containing the instructions for execution of **rmail** on the remote system.

Execute (*X*.) Files. When a remote system calls in with a request for command execution, an *execute* file with the prefix *X.* is created. This file contains instructions for **uuxqt**. It is named similarly to work and data files, however, inasmuch as it is created by the **uucico** from the other system, its job number won't match up with any work file on your system. When someone on your system makes an execute request, a data file (D.*xxxx*) is created. It contains the text of what will become the execute file on the remote system.

Temporary (*TM*) Files. As execute requests are actually being processed by **uuxqt**, additional temporary files are created in a hidden subdirectory called *.XQTDIR*.

You will also see files with the prefix *TM*. These are temporary files that hold data while a file is being transferred from another system.

Once the transfer is complete, **uucico** transfers the contents of the temporary file (which can contain data for more than one transferred file) to the requested destination, or to the public directory if the destination is not accessible.

Lock (*LCK..*) Files. Files beginning with the prefix *LCK..* are *lock files*. **uucico** and **cu** create these files to make sure that no other UUCP process attempts to call the same system or to use the same device while it is in use.

Status (*STST.*) Files. Status files begin with the prefix *STST.* followed by the name of a remote system. It contains the current status of a transfer request. Its existence prevents **uucico** from attempting to retry the remote system until a specified amount of time has elapsed.

Spool Directory

BNU

In BNU, the spool directory classifies most of its information in subdirectories. Work files, data files and execute files are put into subdirectories named for the system that the requests they contain are to or from. Status files are kept in a hidden subdirectory called .*Status*, and temporary (TM) files in a hidden subdirectory called .*Workspace*.

The table below shows the directory structure for BNU on the 3B2.

Table B-1: BNU Directory Structure

Directory	Description
/usr/spool/uucp/	
.Admin	Administrative files
.Corrupt	Corrupt work and execute files that could not be processed
.Log	Log files
.Old	Old log files
.Sequence	System sequence numbers
.Status	System status files
.Workspace	UUCP temporary workspace area
.Xqtdir	Remote executions
system1	Directories containing
system2	files to/from the
system3	specific systems
uucico	Directory of **uucico** execution logs
uucp	Directory of **uucp** request logs
/usr/spool/uucp/.Log	
uux	Directory of **uux** request logs
uuxqt	Directory of **uuxqt** request logs, or remote commands executions on the local system

Because of the revised directory structure, the file names for some of the temporary files have been simplified as well. For example, system status files are simply given the name of the called system, without the STST. prefix. We will continue to use the Version 2 names, but you should be aware that they may be different in a BNU system.

Spool Directory

BSD 4.3

In Berkeley 4.3 (which has a modified Version 2 UUCP), the spool directory has also been divided into a number of subdirectories. In addition, system status files are kept in a subdirectory, and corrupted work or execute files that couldn't be processed are placed in a subdirectory called CORRUPT. When compiling the software, it is possible to set up a subdirectory (called LCK) for lock files as well.

Logfiles

The spool directory also contains a number of logfiles that record the status messages for attempted transfers and remote executions. Because the spool directory was reorganized in BNU, these files are named differently in the two versions. Table B-2 shows the location of some of the relevant files. (All pathnames are relative to */usr/spool/uucp*.)

Table B-2: Location of Log and Status Files

File	Version 2	BNU
Error log	*ERRLOG*	*.Admin/errors*
Log file	*LOGFILE*	*.Logs/*system
Status file	*STST*.system	*.Status/*system

C

Status Messages

The following messages may appear in the status file:

ASSERT ERROR

> ASSERT error occurred. Message is stored in *ERRLOG* (Version 2) or *Admin/errors* (BNU).

AUTODIAL (*dev*: Interrupted system call)

> Modem is in use.

BAD LOGIN/MACHINE COMBINATION

> The node name and/or login name used by the calling machine aren't permitted in the *Permissions* file. (BNU)

BAD LOGIN/PASSWORD

> The login for the given machine failed. It could be a wrong login/password, wrong number, a very slow machine, or failure in getting through the chat script.

BAD READ

uucico could not read/write to a device.

BAD SEQUENCE CHECK

If an *SQFILE* (Version 2) is used between systems, the sequence numbers do not match.

CALLBACK REQUIRED

The remote system has to call back.

CAN NOT CALL (SYSTEM STATUS)

Call failed due to local system error; probably a local System Status file.

CAN'T ACCESS FILE

Either the device doesn't exist, or the permissions are wrong. (BNU)

DEVICE FAILED

The open (2) of the device failed. (BNU)

DEVICE LOCKED

The requested device is being used. (BNU)

DIAL FAILED

The remote system did not answer. It could be a bad dialer or the wrong phone number. It could also be that **uucp** has lost ownership of the dialout device, or that the dialout device is in use.

DIALER SCRIPT FAILED

The script in the *Dialers* file was not negotiated successfully. (BNU)

FAILED (call to *system*)

The negotiations with the modem failed. Probably a problem with an entry in the *L-devices* (Version 2) or *Devices* (BNU) file.

FAILED (conversation complete)

The conversation failed after successful startup. This usually means one side went down, the program aborted, or the line just hung up.

FAILED (DIRECT LINE OPEN *tty#*)
> Opening of the device failed.

HANDSHAKE FAILED (LCK)
> Lock file exists for the system or device.

LOGIN FAILED
> The login for the given machine failed. It could be a wrong login/password, wrong number, a very slow machine, or failure in getting through the chat script. (BNU)

NO CALL (MAX RECALLS)
> The maximum number of call attempts that can be made has been reached, but could not complete the call. Remove the *STST* file for further calls.

NO CALL (RETRY TIME NOT REACHED)
> Default time for the System Status file has not been reached. Remove this file if you want **uucico** to try again soon.

NO DEVICES AVAILABLE
> There may be no valid device for calling the system. Check that the device named in *Systems* corresponds to an entry in *Devices*. (BNU)

OK
> Things are working perfectly.

REMOTE DOES NOT KNOW ME
> The remote system doesn't have the name of your system in its *Systems* file. (BNU)

REMOTE HAS A LCK FILE FOR ME
> The remote file may be trying to call you, or may have a lock file left over from a previous attempt. (BNU)

REMOTE REJECT AFTER LOGIN
> Your system logged in, but had insufficient permissions on the remote system. (BNU)

REMOTE REJECT, UNKNOWN MESSAGE
The remote system rejected your call, with a non-standard message. The remote may be running a hacked UUCP implementation. (BNU)

SUCCEEDED (call to *system*)
Self-explanatory.

SYSTEM NOT IN Systems
One of your users made a request for a system not in your *Systems* file. (BNU)

TALKING
A conversation is currently in progress.

TIMEOUT (*system*)
Other system didn't answer within a set period of time. Depending on the chat script, **uucico** may keep trying and still get through.

WRONG MACHINE NAME
The machine we just called is using a different name than the one we called it by. (BNU)

D

List of Newsgroups

The following list contains the official names and descriptions of Usenet newsgroups as found in the file */usr/lib/news/newsgroups*. This list reflects the available newsgroups as of summer 1990.

alt.activism	Activities for activists.
alt.aquaria	The aquarium and related as a hobby.
alt.atheism	People without religious holidays.
alt.bbs	Computer BBS systems and software.
alt.callahans	Callahan's Bar for puns and fellowship.
alt.co-ops	Discussion about co-operatives.

alt.cobol	Programming for the old-fashioned.
alt.config	Alternative subnet discussions and connectivity.
alt.conspiracy	Be paranoid—they're out to get you.
alt.cosuard	Council of Sysops and Users Against Rate Discrimination.
alt.cult-movies	Movies with a cult following (e.g., Rocky Horror Picture Show)
alt.cyb-sys	Cybernetic systems.
alt.cyberpunk	High-tech low-life.
alt.cyberpunk.tech	Cyberspace and Cyberpunk technology.
alt.drugs	Recreational pharmaceuticals and related flames.
alt.exotic-music	Exotic music discussions.
alt.fan.dave_barry	Electronic fan club for humorist Dave Barry.
alt.fan.mike-jittlov	Mike Jittlov Fandom.
alt.fandom.cons	CONS fandom.
alt.fandom.misc	Misc fandom.
alt.fax	Faxing documents—protocols, equipment, etc.
axing	Documents—protocols, equipment, etc.
alt.fishing	Fishing as a hobby and sport.
alt.flame	Alternative, literate, pithy, succinct screaming.
alt.folklore.computers	Stories & anecdotes about computers (some true!).

alt.fractals	Fractals in math, graphics, and art.
alt.gourmand	Recipes and cooking info. (Moderated)
alt.hypertext	Discussion of hypertext—uses, transport, etc.
alt.individualism	Philosophies where individual rights are paramount.
alt.kids-talk	A place for the pre-college set on the net.
alt.msdos.programmer	For the serious MS/DOS programmer (no "For Sale" ads).
alt.mud	Discussion of Multi-user dungeon programs.
alt.pagan	Discussions about paganism & religion.
alt.peeves	Discussion of peeves and related.
alt.postmodern	Postmodernism, semiotics, deconstruction, and the like.
alt.prose	Postings of original writings, fictional and otherwise.
alt.prose.d	Discussions about postings in alt.prose.
alt.recovery	12-step groups (such as AA, ACA, GA, etc)
alt.religion.computers	People who believe computing is "real life."
alt.restaurants	Serious consideration of the art of restauranting.
alt.rhode_island	Discussion of the great little state.
alt.rock-n-roll	Counterpart to alt.sex and alt.drugs ....
alt.rock-n-roll.metal	For the headbangers on the net.

alt.romance	Discussion about the romantic side of love.
alt.sewing	Sewing, tailoring, and costuming.
alt.sex	Postings of a prurient nature.
alt.sex.bondage	Postings about dominance/submission.
alt.skate	For skateboarders
alt.skinheads	The skinhead culture/anti-culture.
alt.slack	Posting relating to the Church of the Subgenius.
alt.source-code	Source code ONLY!
alt.sources	Alternative source code, unmoderated. Caveat Emptor.
alt.sources.amiga	Technically-oriented Amiga sources.
alt.sources.d	Discussion of posted sources.
alt.sources.index	Pointers to source code in alt.sources. (Moderated)
alt.sources.patches	Reposted patches from non-.bugs groups.
alt.sys.sun	Unmoderated Sun workstation computers.
alt.test	Alternative subnetwork testing.
alt.tv.prisoner	Number 6.
comp.ai	Artificial intelligence discussions.
comp.ai.digest	Artificial Intelligence discussions. (Moderated)
comp.ai.edu	Applications of Artificial Intelligence to Education.

comp.ai.neural-nets	All aspects of neural networks.
comp.ai.nlang-know-rep	Natural Language and Knowledge Representation. (Moderated)
comp.ai.shells	Artificial intelligence applied to shells. (Moderated)
comp.ai.vision	Artificial Intelligence Vision Research. (Moderated)
comp.arch	Computer architecture.
comp.archives	Descriptions of public access archives. (Moderated)
comp.binaries.amiga	Encoded public domain programs in binary. (Moderated)
comp.binaries.apple2	Binary-only postings for the Apple II computer.
comp.binaries.atari.st	Binary-only postings for the Atari ST. (Moderated)
comp.binaries.ibm.pc	Binary-only postings for IBM PC/MS-DOS. (Moderated)
comp.binaries.ibm.pc.d	Discussions about IBM/PC binary postings.
comp.binaries.mac	Encoded Macintosh programs in binary. (Moderated)
comp.binaries.os2	Binaries for use under the OS/2 ABI. (Moderated)
comp.bugs.2bsd	Reports of UNIX version 2BSD-related bugs.
comp.bugs.4bsd	Reports of UNIX version 4BSD related bugs.
comp.bugs.4bsd.ucb-fixes	Bug reports/fixes for BSD Unix. (Moderated)

comp.bugs.misc	General UNIX bug reports and fixes (including V7, uucp)
comp.bugs.sys5	Reports of USG (System III, V, etc.) bugs.
comp.cog-eng	Cognitive engineering.
comp.compilers	Compiler construction, theory, etc. (Moderated)
comp.databases	Database and data management issues and theory.
comp.dcom.lans	Local area network hardware and software.
comp.dcom.lans.hyperchannel	Hyperchannel networks within an IP network.
comp.dcom.lans.v2lni	Proteon Pronet/V2LNI Ring networks.
comp.dcom.modems	Data communications hardware and software.
comp.dcom.sys.cisco	Info on Cisco routers and bridges.
comp.dcom.telecom	Telecommunications digest. (Moderated)
comp.doc	Archived public-domain documentation. (Moderated)
comp.doc.techreports	Lists of technical reports. (Moderated)
comp.dsp	Digital Signal Processing using computers.
comp.editors	Topics related to computerized text editing.
comp.edu	Computer science education.
comp.edu.composition	Writing instruction in computer-based classrooms.

comp.emacs	EMACS editors of different flavors.
comp.fonts	Typefonts—design, conversion, use, etc.
comp.graphics	Computer graphics, art, animation, image processing.
comp.graphics.digest	Graphics software, hardware, theory, etc. (Moderated)
comp.groupware	Hardware and software for facilitating group interaction.
comp.infosystems	Any discussion about information systems.
comp.ividedisc	Interactive videodiscs—uses, potential, etc.
comp.lang.ada	Discussion about Ada.
comp.lang.apl	Discussion about APL.
comp.lang.asm370	Programming in IBM System/370 Assembly Language.
comp.lang.c	Discussion about C.
comp.lang.c++	The object-oriented C++ language.
comp.lang.clu	The CLU language and related topics. (Moderated)
comp.lang.eiffel	The object-oriented Eiffel language.
comp.lang.forth	Discussion about Forth.
comp.lang.forth.mac	The CSI MacForth programming environment.
comp.lang.fortran	Discussion about FORTRAN.
comp.lang.functional	Discussion about functional languages.
comp.lang.icon	Topics related to the ICON programming language.

comp.lang.idl	IDL (Interface Description Language) related topics.
comp.lang.lisp	Discussion about LISP.
comp.lang.lisp.franz	The Franz Lisp programming language.
comp.lang.lisp.x	The XLISP language system.
comp.lang.misc	Different computer languages not specifically listed.
comp.lang.modula2	Discussion about Modula-2.
comp.lang.pascal	Discussion about Pascal.
comp.lang.perl	Discussion of Larry Wall's Perl system.
comp.lang.postscript	The PostScript Page Description Language.
comp.lang.prolog	Discussion about PROLOG.
comp.lang.rexx	The REXX command language.
comp.lang.scheme	The Scheme Programming language.
comp.lang.scheme.c	The Scheme language environment.
comp.lang.sigplan	Info and announcements from ACM SIGPLAN. (Moderated)
comp.lang.smalltalk	Discussion about Smalltalk 80.
comp.lang.visual	Visual programming languages.
comp.laser-printers	Laser printers, hardware and software. (Moderated)
comp.lsi	Large scale integrated circuits.
comp.lsi.cad	Electrical Computer Aided Design.
comp.mail.elm	Discussion and fixes for ELM mail system.

comp.mail.headers	Gatewayed from the Internet header-people list.
comp.mail.maps	Various maps, including UUCP maps. (Moderated)
comp.mail.mh	The UCI version of the Rand Message Handling system.
comp.mail.misc	General discussions about computer mail.
comp.mail.multi-media	Multimedia Mail.
comp.mail.mush	The Mail User's Shell (MUSH).
comp.mail.sendmail	Configuring and using the BSD sendmail agent.
comp.mail.uucp	Mail in the uucp network environment.
comp.misc	General topics about computers not covered elsewhere.
comp.music	Applications of computers in music research.
comp.newprod	Announcements of new products of interest. (Moderated)
comp.object	Object-oriented programming and languages.
comp.org.decus	DEC Users' Society newsgroup.
comp.org.fidonet	FidoNews digest, official news of FidoNet Assoc. (Moderated)
comp.org.ieee	Issues and announcements about the IEEE and its members.
comp.org.usenix	USENIX Association events and announcements.
comp.org.usenix.roomshare	Finding lodging during Usenix conferences.

comp.org.usrgroup	News and discussion about and from the /usr/group organization.
comp.os.aos	Topics related to Data General's AOS/VS.
comp.os.cpm	Discussion about the CP/M operating system.
comp.os.cpm.amethyst	Discussion of Amethyst, CP/M-80 software package.
comp.os.eunice	The SRI Eunice system.
comp.os.mach	The MACH OS from CMU and other places.
comp.os.minix	Discussion of Tanenbaum's MINIX system.
comp.os.misc	General OS-oriented discussion not carried elsewhere.
comp.os.os2	Technical discussions of the OS/2 system and API.
comp.os.os9	Discussions about the OS/9 operating system.
comp.os.research	Operating systems and related areas. (Moderated)
comp.os.rsts	Topics related to the PDP-11 RSTS/E operating system.
comp.os.v	The V distributed operating system from Stanford.
comp.os.vms	DEC's VAX line of computers and VMS.
comp.os.xinu	The XINU operating system from Purdue (D. Comer).

comp.parallel	Massively parallel hardware/software. (Moderated)
comp.periphs	Peripheral devices.
comp.periphs.printers	Information on printers.
comp.periphs.scsi	Discussion of SCSI-based peripheral devices.
comp.protocols.appletalk	Applebus hardware and software.
comp.protocols.ibm	Networking with IBM mainframes.
comp.protocols.iso	The ISO protocol stack.
comp.protocols.iso.dev-environ	The ISO Development Environment.
comp.protocols.iso.x400	400 mail protocol discussions. (Moderated)
comp.protocols.iso.x400.gateway	X400 mail gateway discussions. (Moderated)
comp.protocols.kerberos	The Kerberos authentification server.
comp.protocols.kermit	Info about the Kermit package. (Moderated)
comp.protocols.misc	Various forms and types of FTP protocol.
comp.protocols.nfs	Discussion about the Network File System protocol.
comp.protocols.pcnet	Topics related to PCNET (a personal computer network).
comp.protocols.pup	The Xerox PUP network protocols.
comp.protocols.tcp-ip	TCP and IP network protocols.

comp.protocols.tcp-ip.domains	Topics related to Domain Style names.
comp.protocols.tcp-ip.ibmpc	TCP/IP for IBM-(like) personal computers.
comp.realtime	Issues related to real-time computing.
comp.risks	Risks to the public from computers and users. (Moderated)
comp.security.announce	Announcements from the CERT. (Moderated)
comp.simulation	Simulation methods, problems, uses. (Moderated)
comp.society	The impact of technology on society. (Moderated)
comp.society.futures	Events in technology affecting future computing.
comp.society.women	Women's roles and problems in computing. (Moderated)
comp.soft-sys.andrew	The Andrew system from CMU.
comp.software-eng	Software Engineering and related topics.
comp.sources.amiga	Source code-only postings for the Amiga. (Moderated)
comp.sources.atari.st	Source code-only postings for the Atari ST. (Moderated)
comp.sources.bugs	Bug reports, fixes, discussion for posted sources.
comp.sources.d	For any discussion of source postings.

comp.sources.games	Postings of recreational software. (Moderated)
comp.sources.games.bugs	Bug reports and fixes for posted game software.
comp.sources.mac	Software for the Apple Macintosh. (Moderated)
comp.sources.misc	Posting of software. (Moderated)
comp.sources.sun	Software for Sun workstations. (Moderated)
comp.sources.unix	Postings of complete, UNIX-oriented sources. (Moderated)
comp.sources.wanted	Requests for software and fixes.
comp.sources.x	Software for the X windows system. (Moderated)
comp.specification	Languages and methodologies for formal specification.
comp.std.c	Discussion about C language standards.
comp.std.internat	Discussion about international standards.
comp.std.misc	Discussion about various standards.
comp.std.mumps	Discussion for the X11.1 committee on Mumps. (Moderated)
comp.std.unix	Discussion for the P1003 committee on UNIX. (Moderated)
comp.sw.components	Software components and related technology.
comp.sys.alliant	Info and discussion about Alliant computers.
comp.sys.amiga	Commodore Amiga: information and uses, but no programs.

comp.sys.amiga.hardware	Amiga computer hardware, Q&A, reviews, etc.
comp.sys.amiga.tech	Technical discussion about the Amiga.
comp.sys.apollo	Apollo computer systems.
comp.sys.apple2	Discussion about Apple micros.
comp.sys.atari.8bit	Discussion about 8 bit Atari micros.
comp.sys.atari.st	Discussion about 16 bit Atari micros.
comp.sys.att	Discussions about AT&T microcomputers.
comp.sys.cbm	Discussion about Commodore micros.
comp.sys.cdc	Control Data Corporation Computers (e.g., Cybers).
comp.sys.celerity	Celerity Computers.
comp.sys.concurrent	The Concurrent/Masscomp line of computers. (Moderated)
comp.sys.dec	Discussions about DEC computer systems.
comp.sys.dec.micro	DEC Micros (Rainbow, Professional 350/380)
comp.sys.encore	Encore's MultiMax computers.
comp.sys.handhelds	Handheld computers and programmable calculators.
comp.sys.hp	Discussion about Hewlett-Packard equipment.
comp.sys.ibm.pc	Discussion about IBM personal computers.
comp.sys.ibm.pc.digest	The IBM PC, PC-XT, and PC-AT. (Moderated)

comp.sys.ibm.pc.programmer	Discussion for people programming PCs.
comp.sys.ibm.pc.rt	Topics related to IBM's RT computer.
comp.sys.intel	Discussions about Intel systems and parts.
comp.sys.intel.ipsc310	Anything related to Xenix on an Intel 310.
comp.sys.isis	The ISIS distributed system from Cornell.
comp.sys.laptops	Laptop (portable) computers.
comp.sys.m6809	Discussion about 6809's.
comp.sys.m68k	Discussion about 68k's.
comp.sys.m68k.pc	Discussion about 68k-based PCs. (Moderated)
comp.sys.m88k	Discussion about 88k-based computers.
comp.sys.mac	Discussions about the Apple Macintosh and Lisa.
comp.sys.mac.digest	Apple Macintosh: information and uses, but no programs. (Moderated)
comp.sys.mac.hardware	Macintosh hardware issues and discussions.
comp.sys.mac.hypercard	The Macintosh Hypercard: information and uses.
comp.sys.mac.programmer	Discussion by people programming the Apple Macintosh.
comp.sys.mips	Systems based on MIPS chips.
comp.sys.misc	Discussion about computers of all kinds.

comp.sys.ncr	Discussion about NCR computers.
comp.sys.next	Discussion about the new NeXT computer.
comp.sys.northstar	Northstar microcomputer users.
comp.sys.nsc.32k	National Semiconductor 32000 series chips.
comp.sys.proteon	Proteon gateway products.
comp.sys.pyramid	Pyramid 90x computers.
comp.sys.ridge	Ridge 32 computers and ROS.
comp.sys.sequent	Sequent systems (Balance and Symmetry).
comp.sys.sgi	Silicon Graphics's Iris workstations and software.
comp.sys.sun	Sun workstation computers. (Moderated)
comp.sys.super	Supercomputers.
comp.sys.tahoe	CCI 6/32, Harris HCX/7, and Sperry 7000 computers.
comp.sys.tandy	Discussion about TRS-80's.
comp.sys.ti	Discussion about Texas Instruments.
comp.sys.ti.explorer	The Texas Instruments Explorer.
comp.sys.transputer	The Transputer computer and OCCAM language.
comp.sys.workstations	Various workstation-type computers. (Moderated)
comp.sys.xerox	Xerox 1100 workstations and protocols.
comp.sys.zenith	Heath terminals and related Zenith products.

comp.sys.zenith.z100	The Zenith Z-100 (Heath H-100) family of computers.
comp.terminals	All sorts of terminals.
comp.terminals.bitgraph	The BB&N BitGraph Terminal.
comp.terminals.tty5620	T&T Dot Mapped Display Terminals (5620 and BLIT).
comp.text	Text processing issues and methods.
comp.text.desktop	Technology and techniques of desktop publishing.
comp.text.tex	Discussion about the TeX and LaTeX systems and macros.
comp.theory	Theoretical Computer Science.
comp.theory.cell-automata	Discussion of all aspects of cellular automata.
comp.theory.dynamic-sys	Ergodic Theory and Dynamical Systems.
comp.theory.info-retrieval	Information Retrieval topics. (Moderated)
comp.theory.self-org-sys	Topics related to self-organization.
comp.unix	Discussion of UNIX features and bugs. (Moderated)
comp.unix.aix	IBM's version of UNIX.
comp.unix.aux	The version of UNIX for Apple Macintosh II computers.
comp.unix.cray	Cray computers and their operating systems.
comp.unix.i386	Versions of Unix running on Intel 80386-based boxes.

comp.unix.microport	Discussion of Microport's UNIX.
comp.unix.questions	UNIX neophyte's group.
comp.unix.ultrix	Discussions about DEC's Ultrix.
comp.unix.wizards	Discussions, bug reports, and fixes on and for UNIX.
comp.unix.xenix	Discussion about the Xenix OS.
comp.virus	Computer viruses and security. (Moderated)
comp.windows.misc	Various issues about windowing systems.
comp.windows.ms	Window systems under MS/DOS.
comp.windows.news	Sun Microsystems' NeWS window system.
comp.windows.x	Discussion about the X Window System.
gnu.announce	Status and announcements from the GNU's NOT UNIX Project. (Moderated)
gnu.bash.bug	Bourne Again SHell bug reports and suggested fixes.
gnu.chess	Announcements about the GNU Chess program.
gnu.config	GNU's Not UNIX administration and configuration.
gnu.emacs	Editor/development environment and occasional sources.
gnu.emacs.bug	GNU Emacs bug reports and suggested fixes.
gnu.emacs.gnews	News reading under GNU Emacs using Weemba's Gnews.

gnu.emacs.gnus	News reading under GNU Emacs using GNUS (in English).
gnu.emacs.vms	VMS port of GNU Emacs.
gnu.g++	Announcements about the GNU C++ Compiler.
gnu.g++.bug	G++ and GDB+ bug reports and suggested fixes.
gnu.g++.lib.bug	G++ library bug reports and suggested fixes.
gnu.gcc	Announcements about the GNU C Compiler.
gnu.gcc.bug	GNU C Compiler bug reports and suggested fixes.
gnu.gdb.bug	GNU C/C++ DeBugger bug reports and suggested fixes.
gnu.ghostscript.bug	GNU Ghostscript interpreter bugs.
gnu.misc.discuss	Serious discussion about GNU and free software.
gnu.test	GNU's alternative sub-network testing.
gnu.utils.bug	Bugs in GNU utility programs (e.g., gnumake, gawk).
misc.consumers	Consumer interests, product reviews, etc.
misc.consumers.house	Discussion about owning and maintaining a house.
misc.emerg-services	Forum for paramedics and other first responders.
misc.forsale	Short, tasteful postings about items "For Sale".

misc.handicap	Items of interest for/about the handicapped. (Moderated)
misc.headlines	Current interest: drug testing, terrorism, etc.
misc.invest	Investments and the handling of money.
misc.jobs.misc	Discussion about employment, workplaces, careers.
misc.jobs.offered	Announcements of positions available.
misc.jobs.resumes	Postings of resumes and "situation wanted" articles.
misc.kids	Children, their behavior and activities.
misc.legal	Legalities and the ethics of law.
misc.misc	Various discussions not fitting in any other group.
misc.rural	Devoted to issues concerning rural living.
misc.security	Security in general, not just computers. (Moderated)
misc.taxes	Tax laws and advice.
misc.test	For testing of network software. Very boring.
misc.wanted	Requests for things that are needed (NOT software).
news.admin	Comments directed to news administrators.
news.announce.conferences	Calls for papers and conference announcements. (Moderated)
news.announce.important	General announcements of interest to all. (Moderated)

news.announce.newgroups	Calls for newgroups and announcements of same. (Moderated)
news.announce.newusers	Explanatory postings for new users. (Moderated)
news.config	Postings of system down times and interruptions.
news.groups	Discussions and lists of newsgroups.
news.lists	News-related statistics and lists. (Moderated)
news.lists.ps-maps	Maps relating to USENET traffic flows. (Moderated)
news.misc	Discussions of USENET itself.
news.newsites	Postings of new site announcements.
news.newusers.questions	Q & A for users new to the Usenet.
news.software.anu-news	VMS B-news software from Australian National Univ.
news.software.b	Discussion about B-news-compatible software.
news.software.nn	Discussion about the "nn" news reader package.
news.software.nntp	The Network News Transfer Protocol.
news.software.notes	Notesfile software from the Univ. of Illinois.
news.sysadmin	Comments directed to system administrators.
rec.aquaria	Keeping fish and aquaria as a hobby.
rec.arts.anime	Japanese animation fen discussion.
rec.arts.books	Books of all genres, and the publishing industry.

rec.arts.cinema	Discussion of the art of cinema. (Moderated)
rec.arts.comics	Comic books and strips, graphic novels, sequential art.
rec.arts.dance	All forms of dancing.
rec.arts.drwho	Discussion about Dr. Who.
rec.arts.erotica	Erotic fiction and verse. (Moderated)
rec.arts.int-fiction	Discussions about interactive fiction.
rec.arts.misc	Discussions about the arts not in other groups.
rec.arts.movies	Discussions of movies and movie making.
rec.arts.movies.reviews	Reviews of movies. (Moderated)
rec.arts.poems	For the posting of poems.
rec.arts.sf-lovers	Science fiction lovers' newsgroup.
rec.arts.startrek	Star Trek, the TV shows and the movies.
rec.arts.startrek.info	Information about the universe of Star Trek. (Moderated)
rec.arts.tv	The boob tube, its history, and past and current shows.
rec.arts.tv.soaps	Postings about soap operas.
rec.arts.tv.uk	Discussions of telly shows from the UK.
rec.arts.wobegon	A "Prairie Home Companion" radio show discussion.
rec.audio	High fidelity audio.
rec.audio.high-end	High-end audio systems. (Moderated)

rec.autos	Automobiles, automotive products and laws.
rec.autos.driving	Driving automobiles.
rec.autos.sport	Discussion of organized, legal auto competitions.
rec.autos.tech	Technical aspects of automobiles, et. al.
rec.aviation	Aviation rules, means, and methods.
rec.backcountry	Activities in the Great Outdoors.
rec.bicycles	Bicycles, related products and laws.
rec.birds	Hobbyists interested in bird watching.
rec.boats	Hobbyists interested in boating.
rec.equestrian	Discussion of things equestrian.
rec.folk-dancing	Folk dances, dancers, and dancing.
rec.food.cooking	Food, cooking, cookbooks, and recipes.
rec.food.drink	Wines and spirits.
rec.food.recipes	Recipes for interesting food and drink. (Moderated)
rec.food.veg	Vegetarians.
rec.gambling	Discussions about games of chance (and mischance).
rec.games.board	Discussion and hints on board games.
rec.games.bridge	Hobbyists interested in bridge.
rec.games.chess	Chess and computer chess.
rec.games.empire	Discussion and hints about Empire.
rec.games.frp	Discussion about Fantasy Role Playing games.

rec.games.go	Discussion about Go.
rec.games.hack	Discussion, hints, etc. about the Hack game.
rec.games.misc	Games and computer games.
rec.games.moria	Comments, hints, and info about the Moria game.
rec.games.pbm	Discussion about Play by Mail games.
rec.games.programmer	Discussion of adventure game programming.
rec.games.rogue	Discussion and hints about Rogue.
rec.games.trivia	Discussion about trivia.
rec.games.vectrex	The Vectrex game system.
rec.games.video	Discussion about video games.
rec.gardens	Gardening: methods and results.
rec.guns	Discussions about firearms. (Moderated)
rec.ham-radio	Amateur Radio practices, contests, events, rules, etc.
rec.ham-radio.packet	Discussion about packet radio setups.
rec.ham-radio.swap	Offers to trade and swap radio equipment.
rec.humor	Jokes and the like. May be somewhat offensive.
rec.humor.d	Discussions on the content of rec.humor articles.
rec.humor.funny	Jokes that are funny (in the moderator's opinion). (Moderated)
rec.mag	Magazine summaries, tables of contents, etc.

rec.mag.fsfnet	A Science Fiction "fanzine." (Moderated)
rec.mag.otherrealms	Edited science fiction and fantasy "magazine". (Moderated)
rec.misc	General topics about recreational/participant sports.
rec.models.rc	Radio-controlled models for hobbyists.
rec.models.rockets	Model rockets for hobbyists.
rec.motorcycles	Motorcycles and related products and laws.
rec.music.beatles	Postings about the Fab Four and their music.
rec.music.bluenote	Discussion of jazz, blues, and related types of music.
rec.music.cd	CDs—availability and other discussions.
rec.music.classical	Discussion about classical music.
rec.music.dementia	Discussion of comedy and novelty music.
rec.music.dylan	Discussion of Bob's works and music.
rec.music.folk	Folks discussing folk music of various sorts.
rec.music.gaffa	Progressive music (e.g., Kate Bush). (Moderated)
rec.music.gdead	A group for (Grateful) Dead-heads.
rec.music.makers	For performers and their discussions.
rec.music.misc	Music lovers' group.
rec.music.newage	New Age music discussions.

rec.music.synth	Synthesizers and computer music.
rec.nude	Hobbyists interested in naturist/nudist activities.
rec.org.sca	Society for Creative Anachronism.
rec.pets	Pets, pet care, and household animals in general.
rec.photo	Hobbyists interested in photography.
rec.puzzles	Puzzles, problems, and quizzes.
rec.radio.noncomm	Topics relating to noncommercial radio.
rec.radio.shortwave	Shortwave radio enthusiasts.
rec.railroad	Real and model train fans' newsgroup.
rec.scuba	Hobbyists interested in SCUBA diving.
rec.skiing	Hobbyists interested in snow skiing.
rec.skydiving	Hobbyists interested in skydiving.
rec.sport.baseball	Discussion about baseball.
rec.sport.basketball	Discussion about basketball.
rec.sport.cricket	Discussion about the sport of cricket.
rec.sport.football	Discussion about American-style football.
rec.sport.hockey	Discussion about hockey.
rec.sport.misc	Spectator sports.
rec.sport.pro-wrestling	Discussion about professional wrestling.
rec.sport.soccer	Discussion about soccer (Association Football).
rec.travel	Traveling all over the world.

rec.video	Video and video components.
rec.windsurfing	Riding the waves as a hobby.
rec.woodworking	Hobbyists interested in woodworking.
sci.aeronautics	The science of aeronautics and related technology.
sci.aquaria	Only scientifically-oriented postings about aquaria.
sci.astro	Astronomy discussions and information.
sci.bio	Biology and related sciences.
sci.bio.technology	Any topic relating to biotechnology.
sci.chem	Chemistry and related sciences.
sci.crypt	Different methods of data en/decryption.
sci.econ	The science of economics.
sci.edu	Science education.
sci.electronics	Circuits, theory, electrons and discussions.
sci.energy	Discussions about energy, science and technology.
sci.environment	Discussions about the environment and ecology.
sci.lang	Natural languages, communication, etc.
sci.lang.japan	The Japanese language, both spoken and written.
sci.logic	Logic—math, philosophy and computational aspects.
sci.math	Mathematical discussions and pursuits.

sci.math.num-analysis	Numerical Analysis.
sci.math.stat	Statistics discussion.
sci.math.symbolic	Symbolic algebra discussion.
sci.med	Medicine and its related products and regulations.
sci.med.aids	AIDS: treatment, pathology/biology of HIV, prevention. (Moderated)
sci.med.physics	Issues of physics in medical testing/care.
sci.military	Discussion about science and the military. (Moderated)
sci.misc	Short-lived discussions on subjects in the sciences.
sci.nanotech	Self-reproducing molecular-scale machines. (Moderated)
sci.philosophy.meta	Discussions within the scope of "Meta-Philosophy."
sci.philosophy.tech	Technical philosophy: math, science, logic, etc.
sci.physics	Physical laws, properties, etc.
sci.physics.fusion	Info on fusion, esp. "cold" fusion.
sci.psychology	Topics related to psychology.
sci.psychology.digest	Psychology discussions and information. (Moderated)
sci.research	Research methods, funding, ethics, etc.
sci.skeptic	Skeptics discussing psuedo-science.
sci.space	Space, space programs, space related research, etc.

sci.space.shuttle	The space shuttle and the STS program.
sci.virtual-worlds	Modelling the universe. (Moderated)
soc.college	College, college activities, campus life, etc.
soc.couples	Discussions for couples (cf. soc.singles).
soc.culture.african	Discussions about Africa and things African.
soc.culture.arabic	Technological and cultural issues, *not* politics.
soc.culture.asean	Countries of the Assoc. of SE Asian Nations.
soc.culture.asian.american	Issues and discussion about Asian-Americans.
soc.culture.british	Issues about Britain and those of British descent.
soc.culture.celtic	Group about Celts (*not* basketball!).
soc.culture.china	About China and Chinese culture.
soc.culture.esperanto	The neutral international language Esperanto.
soc.culture.french	French culture, history, and related discussions.
soc.culture.german	Discussions about German culture and history.
soc.culture.greek	Group about Greeks.
soc.culture.hongkong	Discussions pertaining to Hong Kong.
soc.culture.indian	Group for discussion about India and things Indian.

soc.culture.iranian	Iranian/Persian culture, history, etc.
soc.culture.japan	Everything Japanese, except the Japanese language.
soc.culture.jewish	Jewish culture and religion. (cf. talk.politics.mideast)
soc.culture.korean	Discussions about Korea and things Korean.
soc.culture.latin-america	Topics about Latin America.
soc.culture.misc	Group for discussion about other cultures.
soc.culture.nordic	Discussion about culture up north.
soc.culture.pakistan	Topics of discussion about Pakistan.
soc.culture.polish	Polish culture, Polish past, and Polish politics.
soc.culture.sri-lanka	Things and people from Sri Lanka.
soc.culture.taiwan	Discussion about things Taiwanese.
soc.culture.turkish	Discussion about things Turkish.
soc.culture.vietnamese	Issues and discussions of Vietnamese culture.
soc.feminism	Discussion of feminism and feminist issues. (Moderated)
soc.history	Discussions of things historical.
soc.human-nets	Computer aided communications digest. (Moderated)
soc.men	Issues related to men, their problems and relationships.
soc.misc	Socially-oriented topics not in other groups.

soc.motss	Issues pertaining to homosexuality.
soc.net-people	Announcements, requests, etc. about people on the net.
soc.politics	Political problems, systems, solutions. (Moderated)
soc.politics.arms-d	Arms discussion digest. (Moderated)
soc.religion.christian	Christianity and related topics. (Moderated)
soc.religion.eastern	Discussions of Eastern religions. (Moderated)
soc.religion.islam	Discussions of the Islamic faith. (Moderated)
soc.rights.human	Human rights and activism (e.g., Amnesty International).
soc.roots	Genealogical matters.
soc.singles	Newsgroup for single people, their activities, etc.
soc.women	Issues related to women, their problems and relationships.
talk.abortion	All sorts of discussions and arguments on abortion.
talk.bizarre	The unusual, bizarre, curious, and often stupid.
talk.origins	Evolution versus creationism (sometimes hot!).
talk.philosophy.misc	Philosophical musings on all topics.
talk.politics.guns	The politics of firearm ownership and (mis)use.
talk.politics.mideast	Discussion and debate over Middle Eastern events.

talk.politics.misc	Political discussions and ravings of all kinds.
talk.politics.soviet	Discussion of Soviet politics, domestic and foreign.
talk.politics.theory	Theory of politics and political systems.
talk.rape	Discussions on stopping rape; not to be crossposted.
talk.religion.misc	Religious, ethical, and moral implications.
talk.religion.newage	Esoteric and minority religions and philosophies.
talk.rumors	For the posting of rumors.

E

Quick Reference
UUCP Commands
Programs for Reading Netnews

This appendix summarizes the various UNIX commands for working with remote systems. It also summarizes a few of the programs for reading news.

The conventions used in this appendix are as follows:

- All commands and options shown in **boldface** are typed literally.

- All arguments and options shown in *italics* are generic and should be replaced with user-supplied values.

- All arguments surrounded with brackets are optional.

- The options should be entered with the spacing shown. For example, an option shown as -l*device* (the argument *device* follows the -l flag with no intervening whitespace) is different from -l *device*.

UUCP Commands

cu *[options] sys | phone#*

Call up remote system and log in. Either a *system* name or *phone* number must be specified to identify the remote system.

options

-d   Print modem diagnostics.

-e   Use even parity.

-l*device*

Use given *device* to call up system.

-h   Emulates local echo and supports calls to other computer systems which expect terminals to be in half duplex mode.

-o   Use odd parity.

-s*speed*

Call up system at baud rate *speed*.

-t   Dial an ASCII terminal with auto answer set.

cu escapes

~**%t** *rfile [filename]*

Take *rfile* from remote system and copy it to local system.

~**%p** *file [rfilename]*

Copy file from local system and put it on remote system.

~**>**[>]:*file*

Start an output diversion to *file* on the local system.

~**>**   Terminate an output diversion.

~**!***command*

Run *command* on local system from remote system.

~**!**   Escape to an interactive shell on local system.

~$*command*
> Run *command* on local system, and send output to remote system.

~.   Disconnect **cu.**

mail *sys!user*

Send mail to *user* on system *sys.*

tip [*options*] *sys* | *phone#*

Call up remote system and log in. Either a *system* name or *phone* number must be specified to identify the remote system.

options

> **-speed** Call up system at baud rate *speed.* 300 is default baud rate.

> **-v**   Display variable settings as they are made.

tip escapes

~%t *rfile* [*filename*]
> Take *rfile* from remote system and copy it to local system.

~%p *file* [*rfilename*]
> Copy file from local system and put it on remote system.

~<   Take file from remote system and copy it to local system. **tip** prompts for name of file and then for command on remote machine.

~>   Copy file from local system and put it on remote system. **tip** prompts for name of file.

~!*command*
> Run *command* on local system from remote system.

~!   Escape to an interactive shell on local system.

~c [*dir*] Change directory to *dir*, or to home directory.

~$*command*
> Run *command* on local system, and send output to remote system.

˜|command
> Run *command* on remote system, and send output to local process.

˜# Send a *BREAK* to remote system.

˜^Z Stop **tip** (available only with job control).

˜^Y Stop **tip** on local system, but leave running on remote system.

˜. Disconnect **tip**.

˜? Get help for tilde escape sequences.

˜s *variable* [=*value*]
> Set a variable.

uucp [*options*] [*source!*]*file1* [*destination!*]*file2*

Copy *file1* to *file2*, where *source* or *destination* specifies the name of a remote system.

options

-c Use the source file (default) when copying out rather than copying the file to the spool directory.

-C Copy source file to spool directory before copying out.

-d Make necessary directories for the copy when they do not exist.

-f Do not make intermediate directories when they do not exist.

-m*file* Report status of copy in *file*. If *file* is omitted, notify sender of status.

-n*rec* Notify *rec*ipient of file on remote system that a file was sent.

-j Report job number of copy request.

-e*sys* Execute **uucp** command on remote system *sys*.

-r Queue the job but do not start communication program (**uucico**).

-s*file* Send transfer status to *file* (a full pathname).

-x*n*   Specify the level of debugging output desired to be *n*, $0 \le n \le 9$. High numbers give more output.

uudecode   *bin.file*

Decode binary file sent by **uuencode**.

uuencode   *bin.file*

Copy binary file to remote system.

uulog   *[options]*

Display status of UUCP transfer.

options

> **-s***sys*   Display status of UUCP transfer by system.
>
> **-u***user*   Display status of UUCP transfer by user.

uuname   *[option]*

List names of remote systems known to local system.

options

> **-l**   List local system name.

uupick   Query public directory for files sent to user with **uuto**.

options

> **-s***system* Search for files sent from *system*.

interactive responses

> *RETURN*
> > Go to next item.
>
> *****   List possible responses.
>
> **a** *[dir]*   Move all files to *dir*ectory (default is current directory).
>
> **d**   Delete the item.
>
> **m** *[dir]*   Move the item to *dir*ectory (default is current directory).

p   Print the contents of the file.

q   Quit. Control-D has same effect.

!*command*

Execute *command* and return.

uustat [*options*]

Display general status of UUCP commands or connections to other systems.

options

-**u***user* Display status of UUCP requests by user.

-**s***sys* Display status of UUCP requests dealing with remote *system*.

-**j***job#* Check on status of UUCP request *job#*. -**jall** reports on the status of all requests.

-**k***job#* Kill UUCP request *job#*.

-**r***job#* Restore *job#* by changing its current status to prevent deletion.

-**c***hour* Delete items older than specified hour(s).

-**o***hour* Display status of UUCP requests older than specified hour(s).

-**y***hour* Display status of UUCP requests younger than specified hour(s).

-**m***sys* Report if system *sys* is accessible. -**mall** displays status of all known systems.

-**M***sys* Version of -**m** option that also specifies time of last status report and time of last successful transfer by *system*.

-**O**   Use octal codes to represent status.

-**q**   List queued jobs and control files along with time of oldest and youngest file in the queue for each system.

uuto   [*options*] *source.file destination*

Copy *source.file* to public directory of remote system specified as destination.

options

-p   Copy source file to spool directory before sending.

-m   Send mail to sender when copy is complete.

notation

   ˜*user*   *User*'s login directory

   ˜/*user*   Account *user* in */usr/spool/uucppublic*

uux *sys!cmd*

Execute command(s) on remote UNIX system.

options

-   Use standard input to **uux** as standard input to the command.

-j   Print the job number.

-n   Do not notify sender of transfer status.

-m*file*   Write status of transfer to *file*. If *file* is omitted, send mail to sender.

-r   Queue job but do not start **uucico**.

-x*n*   Set level of debugging output to be *n*, $0 \leq n \leq 9$.

Programs for Reading Netnews

The **vnews** and **readnews** programs are two programs invoked to read news on the net. They have the following command line options in common:

-n *newsgroups*   Show only articles in *newsgroups*. If you specify more than one newsgroup, groups in the list should be separated by spaces, not commas.

-t *titles*   Show only articles containing *titles*. You don't need to remember the exact title. *titles* is any string that is contained the title, so you can search for a keyword or two, if you like.

-a [*date*]	Show only articles more recent than *date*. *date* should be in *mm/dd/yy* format.
-x	Ignore the list of already-read articles in *.newsrc*. That is, show all news, even if it has previously been read. This option is generally used together with one of the other options.

vnews

commands

!	Shell escape.
+ [*n*]	Forward *n* articles.
- [*n*]	Backward *n* articles.
<	Select article by ID.
?	Display help screen.
A#	Select article by number.
b	Back up to previous article.
c	Cancel reply.
D	Decryption (rot 13).
e	Escape without marking article.
ESC-**r**	Reply directly by mail.
f	Post follow-up article.
H	Display fully descriptive header.
h	Display header only.
K	Mark remaining articles as read.
l	Display article.
m	Move to next article in digest.
N	Move to next or specified newsgroup.
n	Go to next article.
P	Select parent article.
q	Quit news.
R	Reply, including copy of article.

r	Reply, using editor.
RETURN	
	Next page or article.
s	Save article in file (default is "Articles").
ug	Unsubscribe to newsgroup.
v	Display current version of news
w	Write article without header to file.
x	Exit without updating *.newsrc*.
^B	Page backward
^D	Half page forward
^L	Redraw screen
^N	Move forward *n* lines
^P	Move backward *n* lines
^U	Half page backward

readnews

commands

!	Shell escape
?	Display help screen
<#>	Select article by number
-	Back up to previous article
b	Back up to previous article
c	Cancel reply
d	Digest article
e	Escape without marking article
f	Post follow-up article.
H	Display fully descriptive header
h	Display descriptive header
K	Mark remaining articles as read
N	Move to next or specified newsgroup
n	Go to next article

P   Select parent article

q   Quit news

r   Reply by mail to author

RETURN

          Display article

s   Save article in file (default is "Articles")

s | Send article as standard input to program

U   Unsubscribe to newsgroup

v   Display current version of news

x   Exit without updating *.newsrc*

y   Display article

Index

S

script
  cu program 88
security
  file system 15
selecting an editor
  postnews command 125
sending files with mail 11
sending mail 9
shell input redirection symbol 11
shell scripts 42, 43
shortening remote addresses 94
Sign variable
  .mailrc file 94
.signature file 127
signing your name
  news programs 127
software
  required for UUCP 2
source file 23
spool directory 137
  Berkeley 4.3 141
  BNU 139
  checking logfiles 60
  Version 2 138
spooling 27, 39, 66
status files 56, 66, 139
  location of 141
status messages 34, 39, 62, 67, 68,
  71
  listed 142
  reading 61
STST. files 68
subgroups
  newsgroups 103
system names
  remote 8
Systems file 67
  entries 67

T

take command (see also cu) 81
  control lines 81
takeit script 83
tar program 98
temporary (TM) files 138
tilde character 33, 37
tilde-dot 79
tilde-tilde 81
tip program 73
  environment variables 86-88
  /etc/remote 76
  in a Nutshell 80
tracking UUCP requests 38, 52,
  63, 66, 67, 70, 71, 72
trailer line
  binary files 95
transferring files 14, 16, 17, 21,
  23, 25, 26, 27, 29, 35, 36, 37,
  38, 43, 96
  binary 94
  cu program 81
  error messages 26
  file permissions 35
  killing requests 41
  notification 28
  summary 43
  to a login directory 37
transferring hierarchies 97
transferring protected files 37
transmission speeds 77

U

Usenet 13, 91, 99
  etiquette 124, 129
  finding other systems 121
  finding out where you are 121
  getting started 104
  network 12
  phone line time 97
  posting news 122
  programs for reading news 104,
    110

Colophon

Our look is the result of reader comments, our own experimentation, and distribution channels.

Distinctive covers complement our distinctive approach to UNIX documentation, breathing personality and life into potentially dry subjects. UNIX and its attendant programs can be unruly beasts. Nutshell Handbooks help you tame them.

The animal featured on the cover of *Using UUCP and Usenet* is a greater kudu.

Edie Freedman designed this cover and the entire UNIX bestiary that appears on other Nutshell Handbooks. The beasts themselves are adapted from 19th-century engravings.

Linda Lamb designed the page layout for the Nutshell Handbooks. The text of this book is set in Times Roman; headings are Helvetica®; examples are Courier. Text was prepared using the *troff* text formatter and the *devps* PostScript® filter. Figures are produced with a Macintosh™. Printing is done on an Apple LaserWriter®.

The hidden Wire-O binding performs double duty: lying flat for easier reading and giving a printed spine for bookshelves.